Navigating in Cyberspace

M W
& R

Navigating in Cyberspace
A GUIDE
TO THE NEXT
MILLENNIUM

Frank Ogden

MACFARLANE WALTER & ROSS
TORONTO

MACFARLANE WALTER & ROSS
37A Hazelton Avenue
Toronto, Canada M5R 2E3

Canadian Cataloguing in Publication Data

Ogden, Frank, 1920-
    Navigating in cyberspace : a guide to the next millennium

Includes CD-ROM.
ISBN 0-921912-85-4

1. Twenty-first century - Forecasts.
2. Technology - Social aspects.
I. Title.

CB161.044 1995   303.49'09'05   C95-932023-7

The publisher gratefully acknowledges the support of
the Canada Council and the Ontario Arts Council

Printed and bound in The United States of America

Acknowledgments

Although my name is on the cover this book, it could not have been completed without the skillful editorial direction of John Robert Colombo who took a mountain of my electronic musings and shaped them into pleasant rolling hills of print. I am also grateful to my personal editor and wife, Carol Baker, my daughter, Lodei, and my long-time colleague and assistant Jim Semenick, all who have contributed substantially to my success.

Contents

3. Communications

4. The New Order

8. Other Trends of Tomorrow

Conclusion

Appendix

Introduction

I don't see myself as a writer or an author. I see myself as a communicator, someone who talks for a living. I talk about change. I'm the apostle of change. I'm the seer of change. I try to peer into the future to better understand the present. As a result, I'm asked to speak at annual meetings and management seminars by corporate executives, businesspeople, television producers, magazine editors, newspaper columnists, and educators and teachers. I've addressed corporate and business groups on all five continents.

In my lectures I always mention that I avoid the printed word like the plague. Print, as this book will make clear, is an outmoded medium. The "digirati," aristocrats of technology, publish ideas on computer disks. To do anything else would be like publishing on stone tablets when print was in its heyday. The wave of the next millennium is to publish electronically. Few people, however, seem certain of how to embrace the future and all of the products that it will soon bring. That is why I wrote *Navigating in Cyberspace*. Think of this book as a tool to take you to tomorrow. Packaged with a CD-ROM, it is part Gutenberg technology, part new technology and it will ease you into the future as you read my lessons first in print, then electronically. Once you compare the two methods of reading you will understand why Gutenberg text will soon be obsolete. You will also be certain about how to prepare for the next millennium.

I have never had a real job. For the past 22,000 days, I have explored the world like a modern Marco Polo. Some of these trips have been in mind, but most have taken place in the real world. Both types of travel have been exciting journeys to unorthodox destinations. I have navigated through decades of change, studying its effects and pursuing untrodden routes to profitable nonconformity.

Most of my life I have asked myself, why does common knowledge, information which is taught in schools, command so high a price? Not only is common knowledge readily available and easily acquired, it is generally obtained without risk. Uncommon knowledge is known only to the few who experience it, i.e.: living through a war, an economic depression, or a crippling disease. Such events force one to adapt quickly and learn new ways to live. If common knowledge is expensive, what is uncommon knowledge worth, information that is hard to come by? My travels have taught me that uncommon knowledge, which is available at considerable risk, commands a far higher price than common knowledge. Why? Common knowledge is a commodity of today. Uncommon knowledge is necessary for tomorrow because it forces us to look at new ways to survive.

People with varied experiences are able to make connections between the common and the uncommon, which is the way to find new solutions to old problems. For example, my first insight into the complexity of computer technology came from a Stone Age chief in the Kikori rain forest in Papua New Guinea. Similar revelations have resulted from my encounters with unconventional people elsewhere. Indeed, once you learn the elegant order underlying the chaos enveloping our world, new perspectives surface and undreamed-of opportunities suddenly seem possible.

Technology today makes the laws and breaks the laws. Failure to realize this can be hazardous to economic health. Within ten years, technology that is hardly out of the starting gate will change 90 percent of our culture and society, as well as the way we think, learn, love, understand, work, and survive. One can no longer depend on big government, big business, or organized labor. Their days are numbered.

Executives often so wrapped up with today's way of doing things are extremely vulnerable. Unaware of how to enter the terrain of tomorrow, their situations will worsen unless they find quick new ways to absorb data — like watching recorded TV news in fast-forward — and learn to make connections. Workers in less highly placed positions face a more dire predicament: they have trouble finding time, among the pressing chores of daily living, to acquire the knowledge and abilities we will all need to survive in the future.

Entrepreneurs and creative thinkers will always be "citizens in demand." Why? They are risk-takers. Like fighter pilots they feel invincible. Even after their business plans are shot down, they get up and fly again. They may get knocked out of action, but still rise to great heights. For example, Henry Ford went bankrupt five times before "doing the impossible." But when he finally succeeded, the world changed. To the thinking entrepreneur, Ford's road to success is more important than the economic gain that ensued. Financial survival is about the game, not the prize. Once you click in a risk-taking operation, economic worries disappear and rewards follow automatically.

The best investment on the planet, in any currency, is your own brain. You must depend on yourself and learn all you can. This book takes you on a trek into tomorrow and will make you wonder why you've spent so much time and energy worrying about how come governments, corporations, and unions haven't done a better job of looking after you. This book will teach you that by preparing your brain for the future, freedom and excitement, exhilarating and seductive, will follow. New opportunities in the vast modern jungle of possibilities will suddenly be available.

Technological advances affect everyone and alter the world in unimaginable ways. For example, the astrolabe, used by medieval monks to measure distances to the moon, sun, and stars, revolutionized the world once it was placed in the hands of King Henry the Navigator of Portugal. With the astrolabe, Portuguese navigators ushered in the Age of Discoveries, and in 80 years Portugal became the world's leading maritime, then economic, power. All this happened because of a simple device, which the Portuguese were the first to use for maritime navigations.

Ages ago, change came slowly and adaptation to new social conditions took years. In ancient times, we kept records on cave walls, on stone tablets, on knotted pieces of string. We wrote on goat hide, on papyrus, on mashed linen and flax, on pulp from trees. But each new invention taught us how to walk more boldly in the environment of change. Eventually, we learned how to run: we invented the wheel, the ship, the train, the car, the plane, the jet, the rocket, and the space shuttle. Every invention has spawned more inventions. The hand-held calculator led to the computer. Our world was changed forever. Again. Soon disks will be as common, then more common than books.

Today, technology is accelerating at unprecedented rates and we must constantly adapt. Daily. Simply by reading this book and then using the disk that comes with it, you are taking a step into the next millennium. I am called a futurist. But if I don't change today, tomorrow I will be a historian. The following pages are full of interesting facts and provocative ideas which, coupled with your own experiences, should provide insights that will help you to incorporate change into your own life, perhaps inviting you to take new risks.

What once took 10,000 years to happen now occurs in a decade. What once took five years now takes one. Big-city skyscrapers, once a possession of pride, are now seen by some as raw material for the ghost towns of tomorrow. But even ghost towns have merit. They can serve as beacons, or they can be resettled. Nothing is forever once you understand survival: today, tomorrow, and beyond.

1 Towards the Third Millennium

The River of Change

The never-ending flow of technology is the history of the River of Change.

Long, long ago in our distant past, one water droplet represented a millennia of time. Over centuries, one droplet added to another, eventually turning into a torrent of drops that grew into a mighty river, the River of Change. Unlike many other rivers, this one took a very, very long time to grow. It swelled so slowly that it wasn't even noticed in the small jungle setting where it was born. Eventually, however, the body of water turned into the largest and longest-running river in the world. Today, the river is flooding the world. Flooding it with technology.

Like it or not, today, technology makes the laws and

breaks the laws. The first use of technology occurred when our earliest ancestor picked up a discarded bone and held it as a tool or a weapon. Someone took a stick, used it to carve a line in the earth, and dropped seeds into the ground. By the time a handle was attached to the stick to create a plow, another 100,000 years had passed.

Even with the passage of thousands of years, technology, and with it, change, was often unrecognized because it happened so seldom. But whenever and wherever it did appear, life was irrevocably changed. For most of humanity, life was altered when the first stick and seed were used and people turned from being hunters and gatherers to becoming the world's first farmers. Technology changed where we lived, how we lived, how and what we ate.

Over time, technology allowed us to do more and more with what we had learned. Society of a sort developed, generally along a path that used technology to progress further and faster than others who ignored innovations. Not all developments worked. Not every one was useful. Millions of attempted changes failed, and those who tied their existence to such changes perished with their treasures. It became prudent to be conservative. Not all toys offered by technology were desirable.

The idea of Time evolved, along with other technologies in the wilderness of the past. As a species, humans moved from the jungle to savannas, while technology produced more new things to ease our travels along uncharted routes. But not all was smooth. Technology and change were still relative strangers and only occasional visitors.

As human beings became more productive farmers, villages were created by using the very items technology had provided. People learned to develop new ideas and products to help their clans. They were the first navigators on the River of Change.

Sometime around the eighth century, technology began traveling around the planet and a new device from Asia was introduced in western Europe. This was the horse's stirrup. Life would henceforth be different. For the first time, man could be in full control of his horse. He could wear heavy armor and carry a long lance. The rider was almost invulnerable. Now when he mounted his horse and charged a village's defenses, it was the previously pampered and successful village bowmen who ended up on the wrong end of the spear. A new game was under way. Someone made himself king. He called his buddies knights. The concept of Camelot was devised. The humble stirrup, that sophisticated invention, allowed riders to build kingdoms.

Later, from the shores of Iberia, came the astrolabe, still admired today for its rudimentary sophistication. The astrolabe enabled sailors to navigate unknown seas, discover other worlds, and build bold empires. The world would never be the same again.

Soon the Industrial Revolution occurred, an event which dates from the invention of the printing press and movable type by Johannes Gutenberg. The Gutenberg press allowed the knowledge of technology to spread far and wide. It

permitted technology to become a racing stream, full of
energy and gaining strength as it ran. Innovation flowed
forth until the stream became a small river.

Then technology began acquiring friends. Gutenberg-
format print allowed anyone interested to record and
store knowledge. It gave information to the great
unwashed, mobility to the daring, and wealth and power
to innocents who had never tasted such intoxicants.

Once the masses learned what the nobility knew, fear
faded and confidence grew. Knights, who often advised
their monarchs, enjoyed the greatest advantages from the
invention of the stirrup. Through their own maneuver-
ing, knights grew wealthy alongside their monarchs.
Civilization, chivalry, and everyday comforts appeared on
the scene. Burghers began to emerge from the peasant
population. Craftsmen and traders began to provide
many items that appealed to members of the nobility.
Life had more hope.

Within decades, more machines materialized.
Technology grew and new systems of learning known as
schools were established. Up until this time, the
schooled were the offspring of royalty, taught by hired
tutors on a one-to-one basis. Now schooling became
available to the children of the growing trade and artisan
communities. In 1480, before the Gutenberg explosion,
there were 34 schools in all of England; eight years later,
there were 440. Information, a technological relative, ran
rampant across the land.

At the end of the fifteenth century, Arab numerals

replaced Roman symbols. Pagination arrived in 1516. Change was tripping over itself in an unprecedented way. Forty years after Gutenberg invented the printing press and produced the first Bible in 1456, the mechanical marvel was replicated in 110 cities in six countries.

Century followed century as tech fever infected pretty well everyone in the Western world. Today, in the United States, the products, processes, and services of technology are ubiquitous: 11,500 newspapers; 11,500 periodicals; 27,000 video stores; 500,000,000 radios; 98 percent of homes have television sets—half of them with more than one; more than 100,000 new book titles appear every year, 300,000 worldwide. Every day 41 million photographs are created in America, and 60 billion pieces of mail are processed.

Technology continues to increase exponentially. In the eyes of some, this means that chaos looms ominously over the future. But this is not the case. The technology of the industrial age, and humanity's pent-up yearning to advance into the unknown, is what spawns more and more innovations. It is our nature to yearn for change; adapting to it is what we fear. Chaos does not loom over our future, only our own fears do. But those willing to think the unthinkable will see opportunity rather than chaos, and fortune rather than fear. Such individuals will know how to navigate to the next millennium.

Thinking the Unthinkable

When the unthinkable becomes commonplace, it's time to consider new options. What's unthinkable? Consider the following.

Who would have thought that the Union of Soviet Socialist Republics (USSR) could disintegrate overnight? That Pennsylvania Railroad, the once-largest railroad in America, would go into bankruptcy? Ditto, Olympia & York, the world's largest landlord. Who would believe that 170 new countries would appear on the planet since the formation of the United Nations in 1948? Who would have guessed that 40 percent of the companies on the prestigious Fortune 500 list a decade ago would no longer exist today?

Ninety percent of all the goods, services, and new technological developments that we will be interacting with by the year 2004 have not yet been developed. Trends already on the horizon suggest that the next decade will make the past look tame. In the next millennium, the 1990s will look like the Age of Tranquillity. Unions will fade by the end of the decade. It's happening already, especially in British Columbia, the most unionized province in Canada. Along with downsizing, global competition and technological advances are threatening every existing job. When the environment changes, everything changes.

Data-compression technology, now in the marketplace,

will change two floors of every 13 urban office towers into unfillable vacancies—unfillable until they are converted into condos. How? The CD-ROM optical-disk storage system can already put the information equivalent of 1,000 300-page books on one 4.5-inch disk. In the near future, these disks will be upgraded to hold 10 million pages.

The first waves of technological change will eliminate not only jobs but also whole industries and entire cities. Before the Crusades, the cities of Solingen in Germany and Sheffield in England made swords. Later, as the world became more sophisticated, they made fine cutlery. Between the sixteenth and twentieth centuries, small blacksmith shops and forges grew into large industries, and these towns became big industrial centers. Their livelihoods depended on those well-established industries. Today, these towns face a new challenge. Ceramic knives which never need sharpening are being produced in Japan. Scissors, too.

The manufacture and sale of film and cameras has been a growing industry in many countries ever since photography appeared about 150 years ago. Since then, professional and amateur photographers have honed their skills and built huge collections of prints and slides. Today, electronic cameras are hitting the marketplace. They require no skill and no film; the images they create need no developing and no processing. Even photo albums aren't necessary. Electronic cameras take pictures that appear immediately on your television set or computer screen; they can be faxed around the world. Some of these cameras also record any ambient sound and spoken comments. Say goodbye to the silent Kodak moment.

All these inventions, unthinkable a short while ago, will soon be commonplace. This means that you have to start considering new options. The type of institution designed for the A,B,C-1,2,3 linear world of the industrial age cannot survive because the needs, structure, and economics of the next decade will not support yesterday's castles erected on sand. A new tide of change is sweeping in earlier and faster than ever before. Start considering what might be unthinkable in the next millennium and you will control the industries of tomorrow.

The New Aristocracy

If you are unaware of the new aristocracy, chances are you haven't been traveling in the right circles—like Internet or the 6,100 data bases accessible in North America and Japan. Or, for life with a European flavor, you haven't met DIANE (Direct Information Access Europe), an information network which can lead you to thousands more data bases across the Atlantic.

For 20 years I have been dabbling in, and dipping into, computer networks, data bases, and global communications. People already competent in network surfing and instant information retrieval have become a new social class. I call its members the "digirati." This new class does not suffer the same apprehension about the future as today's government bureaucrats, corporate managers, and academics.

A new picture is quickly coming into focus. Bureaucratic elites are being relegated to the past. Members of the new aristocracy have a photonic glow; its leaders are basking in a world where everything travels at the speed of light. The advance wave of the new aristocracy follow the crystal lane, where photons move through tunnels of glass, pass through one another and never collide.

Two thousand of the workers at Bill Gates's Microsoft organization have become millionaires in the last five years. Most of these new millionaires keep working. Why? Because their jobs are so much fun. Not long ago, these aristocrats were young kids in sneakers and jeans. In less than a decade, they wrote the rules for future financial survival: have a positive attitude, keep an open mind, and acquire new skills.

The new aristocracy live in a land called cyberspace, an imaginary series of worlds that really exist, as contradictory as this may sound. The term "cyberspace" was coined by Vancouver science-fiction writer William Gibson who used it in his 1984 novel *Neuromancer*. Cyberspace is a populous, vast, and exciting realm which knows no boundaries. In the future, unless you are capable of checking it out in cyberspace, you'll never know what's happening. While it is a place that cannot be seen directly, we know cyberspace exists from what grows there. The treasures of cyberspace draw people in droves. Many "cybernauts" are willing to part with large amounts of real money, earned in their older world, to have, to hold, and to experience treasures from cyberspace. They are the new Marco Polos who have seen future reality.

The majority of the new elite have been the last to realize that today they belong to the "in" group. Yesterday's high-school nerd is now a key player in the new global game. Once upon a time, cities, provinces, and countries tracked large corporations and tried to entice them into opening plants in their regions. Today, those same entities now search for bright, enterprising cerebral athletes. Wizards of the keyboard, along with silicon sailors who are able to ride bizarre winds and create multimedia productions are now commodities in demand.

Members of the new aristocracy know the latest recipe for success. It goes like this: take eight cents' worth of plastic beads, melt and flatten them into a thin pancake, cover the disk with silver or gold metallic material, and load on pictures, sound, color, and lots more; then package it and sell it for $20, $200, or $2,000 to a world hungry for such treasures of the new age. Today's digirati are modern Columbuses, Magellans, and Vasco da Gamas.

Like explorers during the Age of Discoveries, members of the new aristocracy are earning immense profits.

Today's treasures, however, are far richer than yesterday's silks and satins, spices and herbs, golden coconuts and exotic foods. The digirati enjoy packages of knowledge that stimulate the cerebral cortex and make the imaginations of the past seem downright mundane.

Elite Attitude

Although today's rush into tomorrow is being dictated by technology, attitude is a factor that is not being given equal time in the current equation for success.

History teaches us that attitude has often been responsible for success when it seemed failure would prevail. British wartime leader Winston Churchill may not have understood the intricacies of radar or encryption, but he realized their possibilities and capitalized on their power. Above all, however, Churchill's enthusiasm and oratory skills empowered him to present the new technology so effectively, he rallied the nation, its empire, and its allies with visions of hope and ultimate victory. Put simply, Churchill understood the importance of attitude.

Attitude is what separates the optimist from the pessimist, the idealist from the cynic, the maverick from the conformist, the winner from the loser.

Governments in North America are burdened with

horrendous debt. But the debt itself is not the real problem. In fact, it is minor compared to many of the problems of the past. The real issue preventing the necessary economic turnaround is the attitude of the masses toward big government. In Canada, the despised Goods and Services Tax (GST) has encouraged Canadians to be financially "creative" and to question the value of any new tax or tax hike. Clearly, disillusionment with government has set in. Even patriotic war veterans say they no longer feel the same loyalty to Canada as they once did. "It's not the same country we fought for yesterday," they say. When attitudes do an about-face, everyone is in trouble.

Disillusionment with nongovernment institutions has also set in. Corporations, universities, and other organizations that couldn't or wouldn't adapt to change have withered away or died. The university degree was once a guarantee of intelligence, knowledge, and power. For most practical purposes, it is now worthless. Even the importance of the night-school diploma is being called into question. The perception is that academics concentrate on the past and are negative towards the new.

Attitude is everything. In Puerto Rico, I stayed at El Conquistador Hotel, the largest resort in the Caribbean. The service was so impressive that I sought out the concierge to commend the staff. She introduced me to the hotel's personnel- and public-relations people. I asked them, "How do you select your employees? What training do you give them?" Without hesitation, the reply came back, "Well, for starters, we hire on attitude alone."

In the next millennium, astute personnel departments may hire on attitude alone. They will find apprentices with the right mind-set and if these people are bright enough, they can learn anything they need quickly. Today's Internet whiz kid knows that current knowledge is already obsolete. The rule is: Let's look ahead to tomorrow.

Internet Explorations

In the early 1920s, Henry Ford startled the world by paying each of his employees the princely sum of $5 a day—about the same amount a prairie farm worker earned each month. Soon everyone wanted to move to Detroit, Michigan. And soon, many did.

More than two-thirds of North Americans now live in urban areas. The explosion of the industrial age increased the wealth of the world thirty fold. The contemporary saying "Get in on the ground floor" expressed the urge to enjoy the new improved lifestyle.

With the expansion of urban areas, the meaning of the word "community" has changed. It used to have a strictly geographic connotation. Not anymore. Today, thanks to the tremendous speedup in communications, other kinds of "communities" are being born, growing up fast, and going global. Now one of the largest communities in the world is made up of Internet subscribers. There are over 30 million Internet aficionados roaming the highways and byways of the new cyberspace community. More than 50,000 people a day are moving in—and that number is accelerating. It is the fastest-growing community in history and the most extensive communications system on the planet. Those who are unaware of the Internet community will become techno-peasants, the modern equivalent of yesterday's workers who missed the opportunity of being employed by Henry Ford.

The Internet is a global village of 44,000 computer networks. Its citizens come from 160 countries. At present rates of growth, by 1998, 100 million individuals will exchange electronic mail through this system, a rival to world post. Those on the Net already access three million free computer programs and files. Citizens of cyberspace are creating a new planetary society wherein time and space have new meanings, national boundaries are largely ignored, and gender and personal identities are irrelevant.

Geneticists may someday discover that as the Internet world grew, and as vast Niagaras of electronic information drenched its citizens, they were genetically transformed, developing a higher level of perception and consciousness. In the future, Internet will affect the way we perceive the world. Today's paper-dominated society will be replaced by a world filled not with books and paper but with fast-flying electrons and photons. The Net will change society, culture, hierarchies, economics, and the way we communicate and think.

When humans stopped believing that Earth was the center of the universe and realized it is only one of many large rocks flying around a local sun, they created a revolution in thought. Internet has started a similar revolution, with an impact so profound that historians and scholars in the year 3000 will look back on us and refer to the 1990s as the Internet Years.

Citizens of Cyberspace

A few decades ago in the United States, the National Aeronautics and Space Administration (NASA) delved into Project Telepresence. Its goal was to produce a system that would allow a surgeon on earth to operate on a robot patient; the patient, however, would have a direct communications connection to an android or robot at some distant location that could perform an identical operation on a human being. Project Telepresence moved swiftly. The child that resulted from the adventure is called virtual reality.

People prepared to navigate the Net, work in cyberspace, and explore the opportunities of virtual reality have a big advantage. They know it's not necessary to sit in a corporate office anymore. Citizens of cyberspace don't have to live in the same city, country, or on the same continent as their employers. With the numerous communications links to and within cyberspace, workers are "virtually" at adjoining desks.

The first known citizens of cyberspace were British software developers. In 1987, they heard of the high prices paid in the United States for software development and started offering their talents at half the U.S. rate. American software-development companies, suffering from a worker shortage in the emergent knowledge industry, began contacting foreign workers, secured samples of their past achievements, and sought proposals and quotes for new projects. At the time, American software programmers charged about U.S. $5,000 a month for their expertise, equipment, and overhead. The proposals and quotes from the British citizens of cyberspace were very attractive compared to those of their American counterparts.

As the computer age blossomed, programmers from Nigeria and Russia soon became citizens of cyberspace. They began to offer competitive services, which caused prices for people with "old" knowledge to fall. And prices for those with the latest in knowledge began to rise. Nigerian programmers offered rates that were half those of the British. Russians with doctoral degrees in physics, mathematics, or computer science charged a mere U.S. $150 a month for their services (an amount that had the buying power of 600,000 rubles, a fortune in the former Soviet Union).

China is the latest country to enter cyberspace, albeit through the back door. China has been slow in the software game because its regimented education system did not easily incorporate the ever-changing training necessary for software programming. So far, China has been involved with the labor-intensive segment of software, such as inputting vast amounts of data, then digitalizing the material so that it can be more readily manipulated. Although the Chinese are paid extremely low wages (three to eight cents per page of data), they offer a 99.95 percent job accuracy. If their accuracy rate falls below this level, charges are dropped 40 percent. How do they maintain such a level of skill? By having two experienced operators type in the same data on adjoining computers. After the input is completed, the software, similar to any electronic spell-checker, quickly locates and displays differences between the operators' inputs. After examination and correction, the result is a single final printout with accuracy previously unknown at such speeds.

By the end of the decade, there will be citizens of cyberspace all around the world. Today, however, as in the days of Marco Polo, only the adventurous know what's out there. The race is on to discover new lands of virtual reality. Those who can creatively manipulate software will get there first.

Digital Transactions

In the past, geography dictated where businesses were established: the sawmill on the edge of town produced two-by-fours from trees felled in a nearby forest; steel and ore were transported from mines deep in the earth to a processing plant aboveground. All this is about to change. Borders are disappearing as businesses go on-line and become increasingly electronic.

When paper money was introduced, it provided people who owned it with the power to purchase things they needed and wanted. The exchange of physical labor for money gave us the opportunity to buy goods we ourselves didn't make. Sometimes we coveted rare items that came from outside our town, our region, and on rare occasions, from another country. Such treasures became honored artifacts in our homes. Life was simpler in those days.

With an ever-increasing world population, local transactions have grown in scale. These days, goods and services worth somewhere between five and ten billion dollars a day, about three trillion dollars a year, are traded on our planet. And every day, more and more of these transactions are being made on-line. Goods and services are sold on-screen. No need to see the real thing anymore.

Today, there is also daily trade in currencies. No matter what price one nation sets on its labor and products, five billion other people decide its value. They do this by devaluing or upwardly valuing one currency against another currency. If one country says its labor is worth $20 an hour, but the rest of the world says, "No, it's only worth $15 an hour in our money," that reevaluation effectively reduces the value of its currency.

As more and more value is placed in export sales, less and less price control remains with the price-setters at the site of processing. Union demands may inflate prices, but the true value of products are determined once they leave the country of creation. Eventually, goods and services from the country with the lowest currency are snapped up (often electronically) by the citizens of countries where the currency value is high. Low-currency-value countries become full of $1.49-Red-Tag-Day sales opportunities to people from higher-currency countries. Entrepreneurs from high-currency countries can now enter and purchase items at a fraction of the face value of their own currency, in a fraction of the time.

Since such transactions are increasingly taking place on-line, experts who have the ability and technique to track accounts in cyberspace will control world finances. Government power will diminish as it becomes increasingly impossible to track the movement of wealth. Soon geography will be irrelevant. Our ability to manipulate technology will play a larger and larger role in determining where and how we live.

Knowledge Navigators and Surfers on the Web

Around 1970, smart, nonbureaucratic university dropouts could afford to buy computers. At about the same time, teachers became more interested in salaries, pensions, and control of the educational system than in the education and well-being of their students. An educational revolution was beginning but no one knew it.

In the next decade, no one will be able to ignore it. Look to the East to see the trend. Japan is continuing to cut back on student admissions at teacher-training institutions. For some time, the Japanese have realized that society is moving from a teaching environment to a learning environment. Teachers who force-feed students are no longer needed. As we rapidly approach the gates of cyberspace, the changing institution of education needs more instructors to teach students how to use the Net. In the future, educators will be knowledge navigators.

At present, there are few knowledge navigators in North America. Furthermore, those in the know may develop knowledge-navigating software that will do away with traditional education systems. Many new technologies which promote self-learning have already been developed. Individuals can now teach themselves what they want to know, not what others think they should know. The next millennium will be one of choice. Remember when we were forced to watch what television-network programmers thrust upon us? The explosion of videocassette rentals knocked network-viewing audiences from 92 percent to below 50 percent in some markets. The formerly secure mass-market fractured.

The World Wide Web, an information highway much faster and more sophisticated than the Internet connection, will soon provide us with greater choice and a better education. The Web is interactive. You have to get involved to participate, hear, see, and learn. Higher-resolution pictures, in 16.8 million colors, with high-quality acoustics, along with animation and soon-to-be, real-time video, and almost free voice and radio transmissions will present users with unlimited information. Everyone will be able to take a trip to any destination desired, make a movie, interact face-to-face and "talk" with anyone else wired on the planet, and do it at one one-hundredth the cost of a telephone call or conventional television hookup.

Theoretically, North America's 350 million people could all be watching different scenes at the same time. In a few years, we could be watching television and listening to narration or dialogue in a multitude of tongues. It is already possible to read in many languages on the Web.

Once I click on Mosaic or Netscape, I am in cyberspace. With the use of Quikeys, strings of commands and instructions are converted to the punch of a single key. With more than 30 million other would-be digirati somewhere "out there," direct information sources are abundant, and among them people willing to share information and give directions to the unknown.

Information networks foster continued learning. Old-style teaching has trouble keeping smart kids in school. Traditional education systems no longer work because they are limited in how much knowledge they can provide. Those who pursue degrees will be uneducated in the next millennium. Those who surf the Net will ride the waves of tomorrow.

Electronic Immigrants and Wireless Boundaries

Before national boundaries were established and guarded, even before travelers had to comply with rigid regulations to be admitted to walled cities, tribes defended their caves or villages, letting in only family, friends, and on occasion the lone unthreatening stranger. As civilization developed, visas, passports, carnets, and other identification papers were demanded before a person and his or her goods would be allowed into a foreign country. Sometimes charges and fees were imposed to cross borders. Moreover, what applied in one locale often had no connection with what was required in another. In many instances this is still the case.

To work in a foreign country, a person faced a different set of roadblocks. Pay scales were often lower for "guest workers" than for locals. So, although immigrants, usually temporary, were no longer indentured labor, they still served as economic slaves. In Japan today, there are third-generation Koreans who cannot become citizens.

But the traditional rules and regulations that govern boundaries are changing due to radical technological developments and an unprecedented acceleration in communications. Ours is the age of electronic immigrants: people who travel the planet through cyberspace, without facing border hassles, offering their brainpower for a price. Prices may vary from country to country, from language to language, and from project to project. It has become old-fashioned and misguided to offer expertise only within one city, state, country, or continent, when the whole world could use what you have to sell. Five billion people are hungry for new technology and data that will make their lives easier, more productive, more effective, and more worthwhile.

Some time ago, the Japanese decided that English was to be the language of the future and the tongue of science and technology. Soon, fast-working translation software will convert any language into any other at a thousand words a minute. Translations will be computerized and digitalized. Creators who have written a book, drawn a work of art, composed a musical score, or created some computer software will find the world is their oyster.

The world will also be open to that other cyberspace traveler, the knowledge navigator. Knowledge navigators resemble the prospectors of the nineteenth and early twentieth centuries who roamed the wilderness outfitted with a canoe, fur sleeping pack, rifle, hammer, and compass, searching for the unknown. Knowledge navigators will replace teachers who are unable to keep up with changing times.

Knowledge navigators do not fear geographic boundaries. They are electronic flyers who, in the words of "Star Trek," "go where no one has gone before." They cross borders electronically and gather information. People with the latest knowledge and the greatest amount of data are being richly rewarded. In the valley of the uninformed, the information-rich knowledge navigator will soon be king or queen.

What is the basic difference behind the years of the horse, the time of the horseless carriage, and the era of the knowledge navigator and computer-power? In the years of the horse, people had centuries to adapt to change. In the time of the horseless carriage, people had decades to change. Today, we live in an *era of change*. We have a weekend to adapt.

En Route to Tomorrow

Times and tools are developing and changing at an accelerated rate. Eighteen years ago, when backyard satellites first came out, I was at the head of the line. Playing in the heavens had instant appeal. I found out, as the technology improved, how a part of any satellite-dish assembly, the LNA or Low Noise Amplifier, could increase the power of a signal from outer space (22,300 miles above the equator) to produce clear sounds and images on earth. Today, technologies are marrying: the television set with the VCR, the telephone with the fax and answering machine. Tomorrow, the LNA will marry a hearing aid to amplify thought waves to issue silent commands directly to ever more sophisticated "smart" equipment.

Suppose in the near future you remember that your lawn needs to be mowed. You will concentrate and command, "Run Program 17." A tiny amplifier implanted behind or in your ear will magnify that thought wave two million times. A built-in infrared signal will transmit it outside to your mechanical companion, Alphi. Well-stacked and implanted with electronics, Alphi accepts your thought-wave signal and processes it immediately. After all, she has control from here on! "Program 17 is a snap," she will reply. This scenario suggests that at a time when everything is related, one's work or hobby may be conducted in unpredictable ways.

Through the industrial era, most people had decades

to adapt and change to new lifestyles. Large factories were built. Learning was based on, and developed for, satisfying the production line of the industrial age. Males predominated, especially in business. Educators, even city planners, zoned everything along linear paths. We knew where we lived, worked, played, went to church and school, even where to park and where to conduct business. Eventually, everything fit a neat workable format, duplicated the world over.

This world doubled lifespans, increased global wealth thirty times, fed and clothed us better, made us healthier, and provided more comfortable and convenient homes. Our lives became more exciting. Even the poorest were better off than ever before. Many learned to read and write. Our machines meant wealth. This world worked well for five hundred years, but now we're on the march again.

Today we're moving from the mechanical age to the electronic era. Most people want the new style, the new technology, and the new benefits. What we knew and once thought valuable is equivalent to how we used to gather nuts and berries, how we planted corn and raised cattle, and how we assembled cars. I like to say, "Wake up, we're crossing another river!" I call this river the Nocibur. That's Rubicon spelled backwards. You can't cross this river carrying old ideas, beliefs, skills, advantages, and prejudices, any more than you can swim a heavy stream with all your household possessions on your back. You would sink. It's better to shed your old comforts and learn how to survive.

In the late twentieth century, computer literacy is more important than knowing how to read and write. Big is out. For both countries and companies, the electronic pathways ahead of us delight in what's small. Those who cling to convention will ride elephants rather than electrons. Electrons can move faster and change direction more quickly than elephants. Electrons never grow old; elephants become arthritic. Instead of specialization alone, one must learn to specialize in becoming a generalist. Notice even the words, the paths, and the terrain are unfamiliar. Stick around, it'll get even stranger.

An overwhelming number of changes will wash over us in the next ten years. By 2005, 90 percent of all the products, goods, and services around us will have changed. White male Europeans won't be in the driver's seat. You don't have to like what I'm saying, just accept it. The industrial age was created by Europeans who saw the advantages that machines would bring. But Europeans and North Americans have done so well, they have grown too comfortable and lost the zeal to excel.

Hunters and gatherers had millennia to adapt into farmers. As farmers, we had centuries to change into workers and teachers. To achieve and maintain success in the electronic age, we have to change very, very rapidly. Those who change first will transform society. The elite of the next millennium will be more highly motivated than we are. They will be able to apply fresh thoughts and energetic thinking to problems and possibilities. They will be people who have never tasted the chocolate cake and caviar of the high life. They will become not merely equal, but superior to today's leaders. In their hands, the wealth of the world will increase another hundredfold.

Future Rules

The Way Things Were	The Way They Are	The Way They'll Be
Better late than never	Better never than late	Minute to delivery
Get in on the ground floor	Get in on the excavation	Get in on the concept
Order well in advance	Just-in-time delivery	Mindlink inventory
A penny saved is a penny earned	Save for tomorrow	Save only what will be valuable tomorrow
Train to be strong	Train to be smart	Become a cyborg
Pay for hard labor	Think or swim	Mind-based income
Pay the piper	Pay the government	Pay yourself
Round logs	Metal logs	Square logs
Country lane	Fast lane	Crystal lane
Plan ahead	Plan for tomorrow	Plan for lunch
Superpower master	World-opinion leaders	Cosmos controllers
Obedient, grateful	Bright, bold, ambitious	Adventurous, insatiable, indefatigable
Stick to your knitting	Produce or perish	Plan your own replacement
Learn French	Learn Chinese	Learn to operate a translator
The Have and Have-nots	The Know and Know-nots	The Linked and the Linkless

2 Business in the Crystal Lane

Corporate Shape-Shifters

In the "Star Trek" series *Deep Space Nine*, an alien has the ability to change into whatever shape it desires. The alien is called a shape-shifter. A video technique known as morphing, a process first used in Arnold Schwarzenegger's movie *Terminator*, allows viewers to witness the fluid transformation of one object into another. In *Terminator*, a pool of liquid mercury morphs gracefully from being a puddle to a human form.

Accelerating change is forcing many corporations, organizations, and governments to become shape-shifters to survive. A massive Gutenberg-era corporation with many levels of managers is like an elephant with arthritis. Its ability to change direction is limited by its size. It has trouble with new ideas. Smaller, more efficient organizations are evolving, born in the manger of change. These new organizations can sleep beside uncertainty with comfort. They can adapt, swerve, and instantly change direction in thought, product, market, country of origin, residence, and language.

Corporations have to realize that their market is no longer next door in the same city, province, state, country, or continent. Today's market is global. The rest of the planet determines corporate worth, product value and even what people and their money are worth. Alienation of any portion of the market induces a steep downward slide. Corporations cannot afford to be arrogant. Confidence often sits next to confusion, mainly because perspective is changing. Today, everybody in the crowd is the same at the start, but those who can swiftly shift into the crystal lane are surging ahead.

Ways to compete are becoming the litany of economic survival. All the institutions of the industrial age are disintegrating. Those that wish to remain intact, even in part, will have to change more in ten years than in the past century. Soon, smaller and more efficient companies, organizations, and individuals will surpass older ones in technological advancement and revenues. The new rich will become even wealthier through more means than earned income. As the new companies grow, a great number of people will share in the earnings, and new shareholding arrangements will permit capital gains, so that immense financial benefits will result.

If there is a rule for business in the future, it is this:

Any law, sanction, or regulation made with industrial-age thinking reverses itself in a communications-age environment. Here's a question to ask yourself: "What should a successful shape-shifter do?" Let me give you an answer: "Move on."

Planning the Unexpected

In the agricultural age, there was little need to plan more than a day, a month, or a season ahead.

The industrial age ended this situation. A volcano of change erupted and extensive planning became mandatory for any business that wanted to survive. The assembly line, staffed by workers in a factory, necessitated educational training sessions. Professional planners eventually came on the scene. Not long afterward, planning could not keep up with the demands of production.

Every change, no matter how small, alters the world. When change was nonexistent or painfully slow, we could plan what might be done next. A plan could be tried, modified, and then put in place. Time was abundant. Now, because change is a constant part of our lives, there is no way, given existing knowledge, to plan for the multitude of technological surprises occurring every day. One surprise can ruin an empire.

Today, my idea of long-range planning is lunch.

General Motors (GM), one of the original authors of assembly-line planning, has been following the same practices for too long. GM's old plans were brilliant, but now, after a $22 billion loss, the company is being forced to rethink things. Chrysler's planning provided employees with health plans, but the company neglected to figure out how to pay for them. Today, almost $800 of the price of a Chrysler automobile goes to pay for health care for people who don't work at Chrysler. So much for automotive planning.

In real estate, the planning of U.S. Savings & Loan institutions has led to their loss of $500 billion. They couldn't plan for change. The land-and-building-development sector threw up thousands of high-rise office towers across the land, just in time for the tsunami of technology. Then the communications age proved that we could do so much more with less—less office space in particular. Corporate downsizing, plus data storage, has made it possible for all the resources of a big-city library to be placed on one 12-inch optical disk; all the records and accounts of a midsize company can be placed on a 4.5-inch disk, capable of holding 1,000 300-page books (soon capable of holding 100 times that amount).

Planning led Olympia & York, once the world's largest landlord, into a $32 billion collapse. Such development firms as Trizec, Cadillac-Fairview, and Bramalea are teetering on the brink, as is the Bronfman/Hees/Edper empire. Planning was once a big part of building such empires. It is now a big part of their demise.

Some cities have hundreds of expensive planners on staff who try to create crises that they can sell to the public. "We must preserve our green space," planners say. "Roads will be gridlocked in ten years. Our cherished values will disappear." But this is not so. Technology will make many of today's problems vanish. Need I repeat all those worries from the past—nuclear conflagration, oil shortages, global warming, ozone holes, and so forth—that just disappeared?

Don't react emotionally to planners' dreams. We are not on the *Titanic*. We haven't hit an iceberg. The universe will continue to unfold. But there will be surprises. Ask the urban planners, "What surprises have you built into your model?" Ask the planners if they have considered what effect biotechnology will have on agricultural land when a three-storey, five-acre building produces more than a 200-acre farm. Ask if they have considered the changes in value of their precious farmland following the introduction of the new Boeing 747-400 cargo series jet. Ask if they have considered what happens when Japanese companies open food factories in northern China — where there is plenty of cheap land, fresh water, and skilled farm labor available for a dollar a day — and food harvested at dawn is delivered to North American markets the same day.

Technology today makes the laws and breaks the laws. Planners have problems anticipating what the next invention or innovation will be, so they are unable to cover the exigencies that will modify social structure. Today, the only effective planning is training for change. Yesterday, the best five-year plans belonged to the USSR and General Motors. See where their plans got them?

How is a corporation to survive if the planning process is erected on the quicksand of change? Learn to walk on that quicksand and to dance with the electrons of the communications age. You will not merely survive but thrive! Learn to swim in the unfamiliar whirling vortices of tomorrow.

Picture yourself as a crew member aboard a fifteenth-century Portuguese sailing ship. You are eastward bound, rounding the cape of the continent of Africa, heading for the unknown. Planning is not feasible. You have no idea how long the journey will be, no sense of your destination or what will be required to get there. You can only depend on the confidence that comes from experience. The Portuguese navigators knew their resolve and their resources well. So must you.

As the world enters the information age, you must rely on your experience and expertise to help you on trips into the unknown. You are aboard a ship of change, whether you like it or not.

Technological Evolution

General Motors was slow to learn how to adapt to rapid change. Some think the company still hasn't. In 1993, GM had the largest one-year financial loss in world history—$4.5 billion. Evolution does take its toll.

Today, Toyota Motor Corporation builds cars faster, cheaper, with one-third the defects, in half the physical space, and with 50 percent of the labor that is required in GM factories. Toyota has converted its factory floors to ongoing research-and-development laboratories where daily change is the norm, not the exception, and where brains have almost totally replaced the necessary brawn of the past.

Here are other examples of corporations that have become technologically savvy to work towards future profits:

• IBM Credit, which leases out large computers, reduced its processing time from seven days to fewer than four hours. The result? A lot less labor was required and the sales staff was overjoyed. Overall, the company reduced the time for complete processing to one-tenth.

• At Wal-Mart, factory-to-shelf deliveries is now a standard procedure. This has eliminated purchase orders, large inventories, and the need for substantial clerical help.

• Japan National Bicycle Company can deliver customized bikes in less than three hours.

• Kodak reduced 13 levels of management to four.

• Franklin Mint reduced its staff by one-third and watched sales double.

Corporate honchos who can't make hard-and-fast decisions are finding that the new product they thought was so hot is, by the time it hits the global marketplace, overgoverned, overengineered, overpriced, and over the hill. This is why government grants are a kiss of death. The easy recipients of such large sums plunk themselves in fancy quarters (with indoor palm trees at $3,500 apiece), they exhibit no sense of urgency, and take too long playing footsie at fancy dinners with the officials doling out grants. Finally, when they have blown away the taxpayers' wad, they find out too late that some small guy in Taiwan has produced a better product that sells for a quarter the price of their far more expensive counterpart.

Picture Power

If one picture is worth a thousand words, will a thousand pictures equal a million words? And what will one million pictures equal?

The answer is . . . a new world.

I am talking about the business applications of virtual reality. We are on the threshold of a new world: juggling images into a fast-moving torrent of animated, multimedia data, successfully accessed and understood only when viewed, and played, like a virtual-reality video game.

Kids once berated by parents for wasting time playing video games will become the leaders, entrepreneurs, and millionaires of tomorrow. Why? Because they have learned pattern recognition, perhaps unconsciously, while playing electronic games.

The world is moving so fast that even as we start to jump on the rapidly accelerating moving sidewalk of tomorrow, we must learn new ways of compressing concepts, numbers, and realities at a glance.

Are such things possible? In my youth, few people on the planet understood the relativity theory of Albert Einstein. Now, a substantial number of planetary citizens are cognizant of what $E=mc^2$ means. A mass of detailed, technical data has been crunched into an easy-to-read formula.

To the uninitiated, the mountain of stocks listed in the columns of the world's financial pages appear too voluminous to decipher. Incomprehensible to some, they appear boring to many who aren't aware how much their lives depend on what happens through those pages. Soon, however, virtual reality will change how we see the volume and importance of stocks.

Consider the possibilities of the visualization tool produced by Maxus Systems International for TIAA-CREF, New York, operators of a pension fund. Maxus found that traditional methods to help educate clients were not very visual or effective. So Maxus took a different approach. With software produced by the group known as Senses8 fed into a personal computer, Maxus converted mountains of constantly flowing numerical data (via real-time wire services) into a 3-D computer playland of moving colored squares symbolizing companies and stock prices, all located within industry-grid boundaries on a flashing screen. The Maxus tool can help its user to visualize the extent, breadth, and width of their $105 billion pension fund, and so help them ensure the growth of that fund.

Experts may notice a group of Asian transportation stocks moving up, and fast. These stocks, colored blue, are easily traceable and the action is clearly understood. Another box of agricultural stocks is glowing red and declining rapidly. Flying into combat action like a fighter pilot, a specialist uses a mouse, trackball, or joystick to access details on any rapidly rising stock. Background on that holding instantly ensures an informed decision. Is the insurance company selling stock in a battery of food-processing companies a freak occurrence or is it a trend that could make or break millions in moments? Long called a game in jest, stock-market manipulation may now be the world's most profitable "game." And the players earn incomes that make hockey stars look like paupers.

The future indicates an even faster game, played in swirling chairs in a financial cyberspace reminiscent of aerial combat, as flying "reds" are dropped or acquired, and flying "blues" shoot upwards, downwards, or sideways, as the financial battle moves into hyperspace.

Training for Tomorrow

Once upon a time, profits went up and unemployment came down. That was in the days of the old game. Now profits can go up and unemployment not only fails to come down, it increases. How can this be?

Welcome to Tomorrowland. Here's the new game: nothing works the same as it did in Yesterdayland. In tomorrow's environment, the landscape is too new for paths, trails, and signposts. There are no rules or laws. How did we let this occur? We didn't. Technology led us into the jungle of the Law of Unintended Results.

Have you spotted the connection between profits up and unemployment up? Let me explain. Governments made regulations that went beyond what the old system could handle. Minimum-wage laws, enacted with industrial-age thinking, made it uneconomical to manufacture certain products or provide certain services. Businesses began to close down, or move offshore to lower-wage regions or countries. For example, many of the credit-card slips that we use daily are no longer processed in North America. They are produced in the Caribbean where $2 or $3 an hour is considered a desirable wage. Financial institutions were forced to find new sources of labor or lose out to competitors who could move faster. They quickly found out that offshore workers did a better job, with fewer errors and with faster turnaround time, than their North American counterparts who were paid from $10 to $12 an hour. The institutions had to ask themselves, "What else can we do more profitably elsewhere?"

Financial institutions also found that in a market with no status quo, untrained workers are more open-minded than experienced workers. They learned faster and increased productivity much more quickly than previously "well-trained" North American workers. Why is this so? Training that is outdated and rigid holds back innovative thinking. Those previously high-paid workers will not, or cannot, adapt fast enough to keep up with changing times. They can't play the new game. At least 40 percent of the population has been ruled off the playing field. Up to another 20 percent is still being evaluated.

The remaining 40 percent have learned the new game. They are among that portion of the North American population that enjoys an annual increase in income. Those at the very top make more than $300,000 a year, and they increase that income by 74 percent annually. Those at the top have not only assimilated the rules of tomorrow, they have quickly amassed enough skill to excel at the new economic game.

Sunset and Sunrise Industries

Since the early 1980s, the corporate world has been experiencing dramatic technological and structural displacement. In the next decade, more jobs will be shed by sunset industries of the industrial age than will be created by sunrise industries of the communications age. Downsizing hit the factory floor 15 years ago. Five years ago, that wave hit offices. In the mid-1990s a second wave is approaching that same office sector. Huge numbers of personnel were required to operate and manage the industrial age. It is apparent that smaller numbers will do the job in the communications-age environment. The communications industry, already the largest business in the world, employs far fewer workers than the auto industry at its peak did during the industrial age. One possible saving grace during this transitional period is that many more industries, albeit much smaller, will be created than in the past.

As people become familiar with new ways of handling work, new possibilities will emerge for the jobless. In the next millennium, jobs as we know them, will go the way of slavery, indentured service, and child labor. The next trend will be in creating one's own lifestyle and work. Work can always be created. Jobs cannot.

As the baby boomers age, people will be withdrawing from the labor force. Japan has prepared for this through widespread robotization. Japanese industrialists installed more robots in the last two years than were installed in North America since robots were developed—in the United States.

Deterioration in the North American job market has been accentuated by the growing inability to be globally competitive. In 1969, only 15 percent of goods purchased by Americans were imports. Ten years later, 30 percent were imported. By the mid-1980s, 45 percent came from foreign sources! Still-inefficient methods of manufacturing were retained by North American companies because the establishment wouldn't allow fast adaption to change, change increasingly pushed to the fore by the rising and enthusiastic energy, expertise, and economic output from Japan and Southeast Asia. Due to the increased number of imports flooding the North American market, government regulations, and militant unions still operating under turn-of-the-century policies, capital profits have been declining since 1965 when they were at very healthy levels of 10 percent after taxes.

Some sunrise industries, however, have a tremendous potential to change our economy. Already such industries offer substantial price advantages compared to industrial-age products. Consider the lowly magnetic-tape computer disk. In 1975, it was considered a miracle. It went through three upgrades, from the original 5.25-inch standard to 3.5-inch standard, 3.5-inch double density, and 3.5-inch high density. Optical storage for flopticals was 21 megabytes, astounding at the time, way back in 1994. Then CD-ROMs offered 660 megabytes on a 4.5-inch optical disk (about 1,000 300-page books). Then SERODS—Surface Enhanced Raman Optical Data Storage—still in advanced development, bumped that to one million 300-page books on a single 12-inch disk!

An indication of future possibilities lies in a sunrise sector like the CD-ROM industry. The CD-ROM is made from eight cents' worth of plastic beads that have been flattened in the equivalent of an industrial waffle-iron. When coated with appropriate software, the disk can provide even larger gross margins than in the past. Here's a question to think about: As we move to the next millennium, is your industry facing the sun?

Laws of Service

Retail service is getting worse every day. Store clerks seem mad at everybody, blaming the purchasing public for the present economy, as well as for their own precarious employment positions.

Just prior to Expo 86, the province of British Columbia started a great new program called SuperHost. The scheme involved training and retraining staff in the hospitality industry to cope with the large influx of tourists and to treat each one with a smile, with personal interest, and with intelligent answers and actions. About 15,000 workers participated in the initial training. Today, Expo 86 is long over, but the program continues. It teaches those who come into contact with the public how to make customers happy. In Canada, if good service in local retail stores was an everyday occurrence, fewer people would cross the border to shop in the United States.

Every year SuperHost attracts a wide range of companies and individuals to its seminars. Seldom, however, do training sessions run without a hitch. One SuperHost organizer summarized the prevailing employer attitude as follows: "Those who have run businesses successfully for 20 years don't take lightly to an outsider telling them that they can still learn something new."

This explains why there are so many large- and small-size companies going out of business. They are failing because their owners and operators refuse to learn how to keep customers in the information age. Turbulent global economics indicates that companies should devote less time and energy to finding new clients and customers and more time to retaining and expanding services for those already in place.

Many organizations overextend themselves trying to attract and acquire new accounts, then underextend their resources to retain those already onside. Figures show that the cost of obtaining a new customer is ten times as high as retaining one already in the door. Yet few companies and organizations are spending anything to keep the business they already have. Then they wonder what happened when it flies away.

General Motors was once the world's largest company, but over the past three decades GM has lost about half of its regular customers. Why? The corporation ignored those purchasers, who could have been its biggest boosters. When GM's old customers claimed they had a legitimate complaint, the company told them they weren't knowledgeable enough to know about GM's modern cars.

During the early 1970s, I was a radio-station manager in Montreal and ran numerous talk shows. Each show received countless calls from people with auto complaints. When I contacted the customer-service representatives of the automobile companies in question, I was informed by the North American car manufacturers that the customers with complaints were "sour grapes" and represented a minute percentage of the buyers. The manufacturers' line was that there was nothing wrong with their cars. Period. The automobile companies were unwilling to address customer concerns. Now they're paying for their arrogance.

During the 1970s, Japan's Nippon Telephone & Telegraph (NTT) decided to go overboard supplying service to customers. During the past two decades, the Japanese economy has exploded. The result is that until recently when it split, like AT&T into smaller and faster moving units, NTT was the world's largest company. It was twice the size of GM, AT&T, and IBM combined. Clearly, paying attention to existing customers brings future benefits.

A client lost costs big bucks to recapture. AT&T is

now spending hundreds of millions of dollars on television advertising trying to recapture the long-distance telephone customers lost to MCI and Sprint. AT&T is even offering up to $100, plus free re-hookup for those who promise to come back. Many lost subscribers would have stayed if someone had listened to their concerns and questions in the first place. GM and AT&T are only two of the big-name corporations paying a heavy price trying to undo past errors. Many medium- and small-size companies have the same trouble.

For many customers, a business's receptionist, support staff, or public-relations team represents the company, not the president or manager who tries to avoid dealing with the "peasants" who interrupt their work day. But indifferent or remote executives won't retain their own jobs, never mind their companies' positions in the cruel downsizing still to come. Receptionists who recognize by name those customers who call regularly should have their salaries doubled. Such receptionists know how to handle faithful, reliable customers better than many company presidents.

The absolute tops in service and quality are the only criteria that are acceptable these days. Neglecting or ignoring clients, customers, and consumers is the closest thing to corporate suicide that is still legal.

Technology will continue to play a large role in our lives, but it will never take the place of human courtesy and personal service. Remember the lesson that GM had to learn; remember that customers will *never* be part of the past.

The Incredible Universe

Boring is out. Exciting is in.

Especially 100 kilometers south of Seattle in Auburn, Washington. This is the site of the Tandy Corporation's latest offspring, The Incredible Universe. Eight similar stores are scattered across the United States, from Hollywood in Florida to Sacramento in California.

Why the modest moniker? The building alone covers nearly two hectares. More and more, marketing is coupling entertainment with information and super service to snare shoppers and help them make well-informed choices.

The Incredible Universe may be the next major marketing trend: direct factory outlets that couple entertainment with information and enable shoppers to make more well-informed choices while served by staff trained for the new competitive global marketplace.

At The Incredible Universe you can find 45,000 titles on compact disk or videocassette, watch 315 television sets simultaneously, including Panasonic's new "GA00" flat-screen television, sit in a state-of-the-art home theater, and have yourself taped for posterity on your own karaoke music-video with built-in voice enhancement.

The Incredible Universe has no customers, only "guests." It has no managers, either, just "directors" handling "scenes." Within five minutes of asking for someone to answer my questions, General Director Riki Tokuno appeared. Can you imagine, with 10,000 people in the store, that the general manager himself, a cool-looking man, dressed like the rest of the staff, has time to play host? Compared to most retail stores, the service at The Incredible Universe makes customers feel as if they've reached nirvana.

The Incredible Universe philosophy is that shoppers about to blow $300 on a VCR should be able to enjoy their product. To make certain this concept is appreciated by the sales and service staff, 10 percent of employee time is spent in training. Can you imagine a store employee who is familiar with *all* the features of the product that he or she is selling?

The Incredible Universe is also a hands-on operation. Guests are encouraged to try out everything. There are no "Don't Touch" signs. It's possible to "test drive" all of the products—even the latest technologies. All this while a disc jockey orchestrates a selection of sounds and sights from a center-stage, state-of-the-art multimedia control room.

It doesn't end there. At The Incredible Universe, almost everything you could want to buy is for sale. Are you in the market for a new, energy-efficient refrigerator? Perhaps one of the 181 models on display might be of interest. (The latest model is a 19-cubic-foot unit with external ice-and-water dispenser. Or can you handle 83 different models of washers and dryers at one viewing? Shortage of selection is not a problem. And the prices are great. A 13-inch color television set sells for $139; a five-inch portable color television set costs $169.

John V. Roach, CEO of the Tandy Corporation, pointed out that The Incredible Universe is "something like the Annual Consumer Electronic Show, a million-square-foot display of the latest consumer electronic products and things still in development." The Incredible Universe is wrapped into a computer network that links the store, corporate headquarters, and its manufacturers worldwide into instant information on stock movements. If a product experiences an unexpected sales explosion, everyone knows about it immediately, right down to the robot on the factory floor. They know all about your desire for a fast, 30-second checkout, too.

I like the way John V. Roach operates. This CEO sketched out his notion for The Incredible Universe on a high-tech chalkboard and passed it along to Tandy's Name Brand Division for development. The Incredible Universe is not like any other retail outlet and it is meant to be that way. It is fun. In the rotunda, big-screen displays, celebrity appearances, entertainment, educational programs, and new and in-development presentations are reminiscent of a virtual-reality fantasy toy shop for adults.

The megastore has restaurants, ample parking, a no-fee frequent-buyer program, hourly product giveaways, contests, promotions, auctions, computers (48 different models) with more than 1,000 software selections, 292 different car stereos, 72 models of cameras, 575 home and personal audio items, 340 video games, jukeboxes, satellite dishes, and enough air conditioners to freeze a farm.

Computer manufacturers run from Apple to IBM to

Intuit. Four home-theaters entertain, two with THX surround-sound and Sharp's 100-inch front-projection television, and Mitsubishi 70-inch rear-projection with Altec Lansing in-wall speakers! Guests with questions can stop by an information-retrieval kiosk. KidzView is a supervised play area for small children aged three to 10. Financial, warranty, and service departments are all on hand for real one-stop shopping.

Is The Incredible Universe working? I predict that The Incredible Universe is the future of retail, with its extensive inventory and straightforward price information coupled with the absence of pressure pitches from uninformed commissioned sales representatives with no ethics or energy.

Job-Jump to Success

"Job-jumping" was once a derogatory term. It was used to describe someone unreliable, lazy, disloyal, and with a short attention span. We considered it admirable to work at a dull, dead-end job until retirement kicked in.

Thankfully, times have changed and the one-job-to-the-end-of-one's-life scenario is over. The job-jumper of yesterday is today's entrepreneur with all the skills needed for survival. As work environments change radically, yesteryear's handicaps are becoming prized traits. One age's street kid is another's financial wizard.

In the next millennium, it will be necessary to job-jump because thousands of occupations are following the same path as slavery and child labor. For years, the official logo of the Japanese Industrial Robot Society has been a stainless-steel gloved robot hand releasing a worker shaped like a caterpillar into a creative and beautiful butterfly. That indelible image may mean more than initially intended.

Today, almost everybody with the possible exception of some union leaders, is aware that old skills cannot command the respect and pay levels that they did in the past. These skills are just not salable anymore. No matter what training we take, its effectiveness will be viable for only a short period, and then we will have to retrain for something else, quite likely something radically different.

One job for life is an old-fashioned notion. Flexibility is the key to tomorrow, when constant retraining will be essential. Tomorrow will be the Age of Task Forces, a time when groups will gather to work on projects and then disband once the project is finished. It may be location work — construction in India, putting out fires in Kuwait, or setting up Olympic sites.

Or creating a movie. Since the fall of the Hollywood studio system, adventurous producers are bypassing the old ways of doing things, assembling the talent and the organization to make movies their way. After the moviemaking process is complete, everyone scatters. The company dissolves. The next movie may use the talents of some or none of the players who were part of the last epic. The latest buzzword for this type of instant rise-and-fall organization is "virtual corporation."

Soon there will be 6 billion people on the planet. Not all are going to be noticed. No one's going to excel by being ordinary. Only those who set new goals will stand out and they will have to reinvent themselves daily. They will not blend into the background. Actions that were frowned upon yesterday and dismissed as brash will become acceptable and even desirable modes of action in the new era.

No one is sure what is coming next. Change itself is no longer predictable, either in acceleration, speed, direction, or configuration. Many new, small companies are finding it cheaper and easier to succeed by just going for it. Instead of spending valuable resources on market research, especially for a new product, they simply manufacture the product, package the service, and then try to sell it. With change being so unpredictable, there may be no window of opportunity by the time elaborate research has been completed.

Job-jumpers recognize that despite unemployment in the fading industries of yesteryear, there is still action in the growth fields of tomorrow. Most of this new energy starts small with a few co-workers, partners, or share-holders producing remarkable sales volumes. Many small companies, with staffs of ten people, are producing $5 million worth of product a year. That's $500,000 per employee or partner. With that output, the company can afford to pay up to $100,000 annually to productive "knowledge workers." And these people are developing the confidence to go almost anywhere on the planet and earn comparable incomes. They are highly mobile, flexible beyond belief, and bound by neither patriotism nor nationalism. They are truly planetary citizens.

Business rules used to be based on the workplace being part of a stable and predictable world. Most executives can't adapt to sudden career change because it may involve a loss of prestige, authority, and priority parking. Executives shudder when it is pointed out that 40 percent of all the companies on the prestigious Fortune 500 list ten years ago no longer exist, but they do little to find new ways to adapt. By the year 2004, 60 percent of companies that comprise the current Fortune list won't be around either—unless their executives figure out how to survive. These companies, their presidents, their supervisors, their managers, their workers, their products, and their degree of service and quality must adapt to the new business environment.

Remember the Book of the Month Club? Watch for the Change of the Week Company. The winners will keep changing, every year, every month, every week, and finally every day. This is the age of the risk-taker. Poise yourself on the brink of chaos. Be prepared to job-jump. Dive into the maelstrom of unpredictability. Look at the alternatives. Assess whether a dull job is also a dead-end one. The only difference between a rut and a grave is in length.

New Corporate Strength and Active Individuals

Large corporations once had the stable, mighty grandeur of the pyramids, unassailable and all-powerful. And there was a time when those corporations on the Fortune 500 list corralled 30 percent of the entire workforce of the United States.

Today, these companies have trouble hanging on to 10 percent of the workforce. Their pyramids have turned into tents. Soon, like desert Arabs, corporations may fold their tents in the night and silently slip away. Should this happen, they will be replaced by millions of small companies that, like a field of wildflowers, sprout, blossom, and flourish or die. The next millennium's corporations will exist in vastly different economic conditions, as nations move away from an industrial agenda.

Municipal zoning regulations were once as rigid as steel bars. Most of them were a hindrance to responsible development, and many of them were simply unenforceable. In the near future, watch municipal councils and other legislative bodies, faced with economic slowdown and chaotic change, ease up. The city that wants to survive must accommodate businesses that offer employment to its residents. High taxes that were once used to bankroll municipal whims are now a hurdle that businesses are not prepared to face. Can you imagine any municipality turning down the Microsoft Corporation— a company in which 2,000 employees became millionaires over the past five years—if it wanted to relocate its headquarters?

The clout of small corporations is increasing. Today there are 180,000 members of the Canadian Federation of Independent Businesses. When the executive of this organization makes demands, federal and provincial officials ignore them at their peril. The executive director of the Canadian Federation of Small Businesses represents companies that will move to new cities if faced with a municipality's exorbitant tax rate. No area can sustain the loss of too many small companies. The political heat becomes unbearable. The winds have moved the goal posts. The new game is under way.

In the past, a government's economic development officers would search their country, and sometimes even neighboring ones, to find when and where corporations would be opening new branch plants. The officer's job was to entice the corporation to consider their area as the location for a new plant or office. Smart municipalities are now taking a different, unorthodox approach to generating economic opportunities. They try to attract not just corporations but highly active individuals. At first that tactic may seem strange. Upon consideration, however, it is only reasonable. If a dozen movers and shakers settle in a city or region, it is unlikely that they will sit around and do nothing. For them, passivity is impossible. They are innovators who have always been active, successful at creating jobs, and no strangers to wealth.

Draw movers and shakers to your corporation or

country and watch the fireworks. Be mobile and inventive and tomorrow will belong to you.

Brigands on the Electronic Highway

In the nineteenth century, a highwayman was a character like Robin Hood who spent a great deal of time halting stagecoach traffic on rustic rutted roads and robbing the rich. Until the late twentieth century, the booty was physical wealth, typically cash, jewels, and furs.

As the electronic highway webs its way around the planet, new photonic pirates, surfing through glass tunnels at the speed of light, are finding pleasure, profit, and peril among the mind-expanding crystal lanes peopled by risk-takers and cyber citizens. An electronic bandit of the crystal lane brandishes a laser beam and issues the following demand: "Give me your ideas!"

Remember the sources of power in the past. The hunter who could cast a spear farther than any other in his tribe controlled the food supply, the tribe's source of wealth. The farmer who worked the earth was in a position of power because food flowed from the land and could be bartered into wealth. The factory owner had machines to produce things that could be sold for money. Today, the skills of hunting, farming, and manufacturing are no longer as dominant as they were in the past. Ideas control wealth because the next new idea can make or break an individual, a company, an industry, or a country.

Imagine what a new idea can do. Consider this scenario: For years, a huge Canadian lumber company supplied the American market and controlled much Canadian wealth through integrated pulp, paper, and timber operations. The company bullied or bought those who opposed its plans, using tactics that didn't always meet ethical standards. Then one day, a U.S. politician came up with the idea of introducing state legislation to outlaw the sale of any newspaper, magazine, or book in his or her state that was made—even partially—from any tree more than 100 years old. Suddenly, the company can no longer ship most of its pulp and paper since the products were made from old-growth timber. The giant company is then left to replace a major market. But how does it do so when worldwide pressures demand that producers of paper tissue, newsprint, and cardboard create their products from young-growth trees?

Does this scenario sound scary? It has happened for real. Such legislation has been introduced in the State of California. When passed, the bill will serve as a model for legislation elsewhere. A thriving conglomerate may quickly fall because of the power of one individual's idea.

In the next millennium, ideas will equal wealth. Like land, jewels, and gold coins of yesterday, ideas will be the riches of tomorrow. Technology will be the instrument that future pirates will use to steal ideas. Those who want to protect their wealth will have to navigate on the electronic highway and direct themselves to cyberspace.

3 Communications

Global Talk

It has always been impossible to say for certain what tomorrow will bring; however, we do have a better idea of what we are about to face than at any time in the past. We can thank technology for what we know and the ways it has accelerated communications.

We know that for the next 25 to 40 years, the population will increase. Even with cataclysmic numbers of deaths due to AIDS, wars, and natural disasters, the human species will thrive. Why? With the population booming in most developing nations, and with 50 percent of that population under the age of 15, the effects of the explosion will be felt for some time.

We also know, in contrast to previous eras, that thanks to the speed of modern communications systems, everything "there" appears on global screens "here" by tomorrow (or sooner). And vice versa. Knowledge of any impending disaster is relayed around the world within hours. Consequently, in the future, humans will line up, with increasing awareness, against any global threat, as never before.

Telex communications held sway for several decades during the second half of the twentieth century. Today, a transmission speed of 35 words a minute, which Telex once boasted about, compared to current communications systems, is as slow as the covered wagon up against a Lamborghini. Integrated Services Digital Network (ISDN) lines and fiber-optic cables assure even faster data transmission rates—up to 57,600 kilobytes a second via ISDN. The latest transmission rate is 28,800 kilobytes, even on an old twisted-copper wire-pair system. That's so fast, the total storage capacity of one of the early Apple II computers with just 64 kilobytes memory would be filled up in the first second of transmission. With the working standard hard-drive of computer storage now running around 350 megabytes, the Apple II memory could accommodate slightly more than one hour of such rapid transmission. Tomorrow, however, that speed will be considered a relic from Sleep City.

Fifty million computers were sold worldwide last year alone. Even greater sales occurred in the first quarter of 1995. With five and a half billion people on the planet, and with such countries as India now having 250 million new middle-class citizens who can afford computers, the global communications market appears insatiable.

That spells faster and more voluminous planetary communications. The Mac Quadra is an example of what results when millions of transistors are put on one tiny microprocessor. When connected to the rapidly spreading ISDN and later fiber-optic cable, future occurrences will appear truly magical. Imagine an almost total knowledge of the world delivered to your home in seconds. Cables are now being installed in Japan and Germany that will accomplish such amazing feats. As form follows function, developments involving ISDN and fiber-optic cable will change the world in a manner reminiscent of the growth of the North American highway system during the 1950s and 1960s. The new changes will far exceed those that accompanied the automobile.

Some people predict that our current 3,000 daily impressions from publications, television, radio, billboards, Internet, World Wide Web, and so forth, will increase to more than 45,000 impressions daily. In order to cope with the constant bombardment of information, we will have to learn new ways of absorbing it, like watching recorded television in fast-forward, to see the waves and trends of events rather than the individual items. In the next millennium, we'll see two classes of citizens—the informed and the uninformed. What class will you fit into? That will depend on your ability to communicate globally using the language of tomorrow.

Satellite Education

North Americans keep talking about low-labor competition from Mexico. But the days when most Mexicans were *campesinos* (peasants) are over. We had better prepare to compete with Mexico's quality and innovative goods, and their practices geared to the future.

Mexico is the first country to provide satellite-delivered digital video for higher education. In 25 Mexican cities, satellite courses are transmitted to 48,000 students on 26 campuses. This means that students are linked with 4,000 faculty members.

Students at receiving sites are in computer contact with professors during satellite-delivered classes. Satellite-course delivery costs a fraction of the education provided by state or provincial authorities in the United States or Canada. "The impact [of our system] will be significant. It is the educational model for the 21st century," says Manuel Caselle, Director of Technology Innovation at the Monterrey Institute of Technology and Higher Studies (ITESM).

Transponder fees, now running in excess of $1 million a year for such Canadian educational broadcasters as the Knowledge Network, Access Alberta, and TVOntario, are a fraction of the fees that accrue with the Mexican system. Why? With a digital-system transponder, fees are reduced by a factor of ten while they double program capacity. The new broadcast system compresses the digitalized video so it requires a fraction of the space needed for analog transmission. The people at ITESM say they can recapture their investment for the entire system within 18 months and reduce costs $1 million annually thereafter on transponder fees alone. They plan to add two more transponders in the near future. ITESM also claims that the digitalized pictures have a cleaner image and are immune to ghosting, color smearing, and the "snow" familiar on standard analog broadcasting.

ITESM has been broadcasting via satellite to a large number of campuses since 1989. Course accreditation is maintained by the Southern Association of Colleges and Schools (SACS). As ITESM added more campuses to its system, it needed the services of more instructors. But the required instructors were in short supply, so lower-level staff had to be brought up to speed. Distance learning became the answer to this problem, too. The main Monterrey campus is the base for the transmission of broadcast courses. Monterrey also maintains a transportable remote truck that can be sent to other locations. For interaction, there are always some students who attend lectures in the originating classroom. Some 2,000 students networkwide usually view each live, three-hour broadcast.

Mexican businesses, including three Mexican banks, with multiple branches, have signed contracts with ITESM. Bank staff currently take training at the Mexico City campus, but once completion of the bank-training network of 200 sites is in place, employees will take instruction at their regular work sites via the video network.

Sounds like *mañana* has moved north.

QuickCam Conference

The last time I checked with a Canadian phone company, videoconferencing cost around $3,000 an hour, an outrageous amount considering the QuickCam unit permits videoconferencing for less than one dollar per hour.

Let me tell you more. The QuickCam is about the size of a billiard ball, and contains a tiny black-and-white digital camera with a built-in microphone and a single CCD (charged-coupled device). The unit plugs into the serial port on any Macintosh computer and it provides effective and continuing videoconferencing for less than one-three-thousandth the operating cost of the phone company's product. Accompanying software allows the transmission of images and sound to or from anywhere in the world via Internet on the World Wide Web. Nothing else is needed. The picture and sound quality are certainly acceptable for the price.

Anyone can shoot and edit QuickTime movies and take still pictures with the same unit. The pictures can be used with any word-processing, page-layout, or graphics program. The built-in sound capability requires no additional input ports. One plug-in provides all. Children can produce and direct their own movies!

What else can QuickCam do? It can create and e-mail floppy videos. The unit allows you to be the star in your own screen saver, watch a flower bloom, see in the dark, take photos with a PowerBook, verify inventory, add snapshots to holiday letters, even monitor the office from afar. (Time-lapse software is included.) The QuickCam can keep an eye on the baby, monitor vital signs, record a video diary, prove your spouse snores, make training movies, and help sell your house or car, doing away with the need for expensive 3-D software.

Built-in software controls let you do everything the experts do: insert segments in the middle of a movie, adjust brightness, tape video at ranges between one second and one-one-thousandth of a second. Audio quality is about the same as on any household VCR. PICT (Picture) files are compatible with almost all available computer-graphic software. Diagonal picture size can go up to 17 inches, and the wraparound frame comes in 15 background materials. Of course, any image can be cropped and expanded.

QuickCam pictures appear in 320 x 240 pixels, in 4-bit, gray scale, 6 shades, with frame rates of up to 15 frames per second. The unit draws less than 2,000 milliamps. Field of vision is approximately 65 degrees, which is equivalent to a 38-mm lens on a 35-mm camera. Focus is fixed from 18 inches to infinity. Because the QuickCam uses direct digital-to-digital video instead of NTSC or PAL, it works on all QuickTime-compatible Macs. One note: With portable PowerBooks, a flow-through ADB Cable ($10 list) is required for additional power.

QuickCam is the simplest computer peripheral I have ever encountered. Moreover, its accompanying manual is easy to understand. And its price is right. Run, do not walk, to your nearest computer dealer or mail-order catalogue. Soon you'll wonder how you survived without a QuickCam.

Picasso

When my phone rings, I answer the television. I pick up my Picasso Picture Phone.

The phones of the future will transmit, on ordinary phone lines, high quality, full-color pictures as you speak. With a good-quality camcorder (the better the camera, the better the picture) hooked up to your phone, callers will be able to see you, your product, document, design, or photo of anything you wish to transmit. The person at the other end, provided he or she also has a Picasso Picture Phone, will see you and whatever else you wish to display. Pictures are transmitted between phones without interrupting the conversation.

You pay only for the call. The picture comes free.

Until recently, it had been assumed that twisted copper-wire pair home phone cabling had reached its limit in what it could handle. But the extremely productive Imaging Solutions Division of Bell Research Labs in New Jersey (they invented the transistor and have employed seven Nobel Prize laureates) figured out how to push more electrons through standard wires to accomplish such feats as the Picasso phone. Since I received my unit, I try not to show my face without it.

Through an adaptive interface, Picasso can be fed pictures directly from a computer, television, or other source. Picasso looks like a standard office phone with a few extra buttons that control its selection, memory, preview, capture, store, erase, and pictorial menu functions. By using any standard television set or computer screen attached to this new phone, coupled with the usual phone plug, any additional expensive wiring is eliminated. With Picasso, it's just a few minutes from the box to "broadcasting."

One of Picasso's most fascinating features is its mouse, which is similar to that of most computers. This mouse enables parties at both ends of the phone conversation to draw on the image or diagram which they are looking at simultaneously. Engineers, for example, can draw suggested changes on the diagram they are discussing. Doctors can look at X-rays, patient injuries, new equipment, or brain scans. Used as a learning tool, Picasso seminars could be conducted simultaneously at several locations for the cost of a conference call — all this at different ends of a city, country, or continent.

At AT&T's Toronto office, I used Picasso to talk to executives at the corporation's counterpart in Shreveport, Louisiana. I had the folks on the other end of the line swing Picasso around their office to show me their faces and surroundings. They also sent high-quality pictures of parrots and macaws which I promptly stored for future recall in my Picasso memory bank.

Picasso is a boon in such fields as health care, business, and education. It outperforms all less sophisticated alternatives. The pictures, diagrams, drawings, or type-style images that appear on the Picasso screen can be routed instantly to a home or office computer or to a color laser printer for hard-copy printouts or local storage. Picasso fills the gap between the fax machine and the full-color, full-motion video. In the next millennium, it will give conversation a whole new meaning.

Technonews

Recently in Chicago I had an enjoyable interview on WCIU-TV's *Business Show*. It was conducted by host Jack Taylor who is cognizant of the economic impact of constantly changing technology on the stock market as well as how new technologies affect television. In the WCIU studio, there is a robot camera that is controlled by a producer sitting elsewhere in the building. No longer is it necessary to pass instructions back and forth over wired cable to camera operators on the studio floor. Instead, the WCIU producer issues camera instructions through a keyboard.

Remarkable, yes, but such television technology isn't new. I first saw this magic employed in 1985 at the Nippon Broadcasting Corporation (NHK) in Tokyo. A decade later in Chicago, WCIU-TV was using it to keep costs down. With robot cameras, interview shows are relatively low-budget operations that require the absolute minimum of staff and expensive equipment. If the name of the new global economic game is survival, companies like NHK and WCIU-TV are going to be around in the third millennium.

What I'm going to tell you next may wreck the day of all sports fans. Would you believe that one day there will be a robot computer that writes sports stories? No? Well, it's already here. The software program that does this is called Sportswriter, and the concept behind it was created by Roger Helms of Rochester, Minnesota. The 41-year-old journalist's initial idea was to train high-school reporters to write superior copy to what he read in the local weekly newspaper.

Helms sent students to cover games but their stories turned out indifferent; his Sportswriter program didn't really help the teenage reporters. So, like any entrepreneur, Helms took another look at his product and then at the marketplace and came to the conclusion that the only thing his program was good at was making its own decisions. Then Helms realized that as a writer, the Sportswriter program wasn't bad. So he decided that rather than enter the sportswriter training field, he was going to produce software that would *be* the sportswriter!

Helms's program, produced on Macintosh, uses the well-known Apple Hypercard software. The system he set up for this revolutionary technique was simple: Local newspapers provide school coaches with a standard form (currently limited to basketball and football). When a game is finished, the coaches fill in the highlights, scores, and team and player statistics. There is also room to enter descriptions of exciting segments like the big play, the long-winning basketball shot, or the long end runs to a touchdown in the final minutes of a game. The form also requests quotes from team members and spectators.

Coaches may phone in or fax in details. (Using fax-conversion software or typing information from over-the-phone reports takes seconds.) Then Sportswriter prints out the sensational local high-school story. As recently reported by the ever-alert *Wall Street Journal,* "Sportswriter-crafted lead paragraphs varied considerably, including one that highlighted an individual player: 'Jody Kosh made two free throws to put St. Francis up by four points and seal the win.'" Every lead mentions game location, quarter-by-quarter scores, number of free throws, or field goals attempted and scored.

Sportswriter may not win the Nobel Prize for literature or even the Pulitzer Prize for journalism, but according to editor Keith Isley, of the Chariton, Iowa, *Leader and Herald-Patriot*, "It clearly outclasses copy turned in by high-school stringers." After two months of testing Sportswriter, Isley said, "We recouped our cost and the stories were significantly better." It must have had some benefits, since 80 newspapers have since adopted the program.

The Infinity Disk

Today, ten-year-old kids understand floptical disks. It's their parents who can't figure them out.

Floptical disks are the latest development in data storage. Known as the "infinity disk," the floptical is small (3.5 inches), efficient, and versatile. In comparison to the standard 3.5-inch disk used in today's computers, the floptical costs $30 rather than 30 cents. The floptical disk drive (with an 8-inch x 5-inch x 2-inch footprint) costs U.S. $400, compared to about U.S. $250 for the latest standard 3.5-inch disk drive. And as with most computer equipment in a competitive environment, prices related to flopticals are dropping rather than rising.

A floptical disk can hold 21 million bytes. Put simply,

a byte is a character like a single number or letter. In the world of computers, 1,024 bytes equal 1 kilobyte. Then 1,024 kilobytes equal 1 megabyte. An ordinary computer disk holds about 800,000 bytes, or 175 of my newspaper columns. The floptical disk is into big bytes.

One floptical disk can hold 3,675 of my newspaper columns. Each column averages 750 words, or 6,000 bytes. If I continued to write 50 columns a year, it would take me 73.5 years to fill up a floptical. It would keep me writing until the year 2066. Let's work backwards. If today I wrote my last column, I would have had to have started writing columns before I was born. The new floptical holds 22 times the volume of the earlier version.

More than four million words can easily fit on a floptical. One would have to spend $300 or $400 to purchase that much writing in a Gutenberg-format book. The floptical disk drive works like any other disk drive. You push in the disk and it records or plays what you command the computer to transmit. The disk drive required to read flopticals can read older, more common, and much lower-density disks. But older disk drives cannot read new flopticals.

The floptical holds such a high volume of information that data backup will be more convenient, more speedy, and less expensive than before. One can label and store data and pictures in smaller units. The floptical also permits the transmission of large series of files via mail at even lower costs than by e-mail or fax. Lower transportation or transmission costs mark a reversal of recent trends.

The floptical uses a combination of magnetic and optical-data storage technologies. For floptical use, concentric grooves are stamped on standard high-density disks. The indelible tracks permit very high data-density and track-accessing accuracy. The computer communicates through a head, much like a record player's needle. The head moves across the media surface but never quite touches it. Air movement caused by the spinning of the disk keeps the head elevated. An optical-servo directs the head to the location on the disk holding desired data, via specially stamped grooves. The closed-loop optical-servo consists of a light source, two lenses, and a mirror. A photodetector produces the floptical's superior capacity, performance, and reliability.

One can read, write, and format MS/DS diskettes on a Macintosh with the Infinity Floptical drive and Apple File exchange software. Third-party software, such as AccessPC from Insignia Solutions, can also achieve the same functions.

Should a computer owner consider using flopticals? That's a complicated question to answer. There is no guarantee that the floptical is going to become the industry standard. Yet the standard rule applies: If you keep up with the latest technology, learn about it, play with it, and try to understand it, then quite likely you will profit from it. Ignore it, and somewhere down the line you may be victimized by it. You won't be able to do what others can do. That's a big liability in a fast-moving marketplace.

Layering Information

Consider this fact: Two floors out of every 13 in a modern office tower are for the storage of manila file folders. Does that seem sensible now that the equivalent amount of information can be stored at the rate of 1,000 300-page books on a single 4.5-inch disk? Even that quantity will shortly increase a hundredfold through a process called "layering" that resembles the layering of paint. It will soon be possible to recall 100 layers of data by using a laser beam that combines this number of frequencies, each frequency deciphering a particular layer. Layering will operate much like a single radio set that can pull in a hundred radio stations, each on a different frequency.

Let me tell you about an experience I had flying across North America ten years ago to help explain this concept. At an altitude of 30,000 feet, I held the antennae of a credit-card-size AM-FM Japanese radio against the aircraft window. Doing this enabled the built-in genius of the tiny device to pull in hundreds of FM stations, as well as a smaller number of AM stations. Such line-of-sight reception is what gives modern cruising aircraft excellent long-distance FM reception and provides the accuracy of modern navigational aids. What will happen when we develop even smaller, more densely packed data storage? The future holds SERODS—Surface Enhanced Raman Optical Data Storage. This 12-inch disk can hold one million 300-page books, even without layering.

If layering is applied to SERODS, 100 million books could be stored on a single disk!

Something else worth considering is VAST, a unit capable of holding 2,000 gigabytes of information. This development, just 40 years old, is about to be history. Expect to see computer museums created at a speed similar to that of the new products being developed! A system of slightly slower optical storage costs only 15 cents a megabyte. VAST does it for one cent a megabyte. A competitor, Exabyte, providing smaller storage units, offers five gigabytes per tape, soon to be bumped to 40 megabytes per tape.

With all of these possibilities to layer and store information, libraries will become the ghettos for the poor. A new multimillion-dollar library, built in the style of the Roman Coliseum was just opened in Vancouver. But the building is almost obsolete. In the next millennium, libraries will no longer need a physical location. Find a viable use for old libraries and you'll have discovered a profitable niche. Remember that it wasn't too long after the original Coliseum was constructed that barbarian hordes stormed the gates of Rome, marking the end of that culture and society.

The Receptor

The latest in pager communications comes in a wrist-watch style and a neat pocket unit.

Known as The Receptor, the product displays incoming messages on a small window, which also indicates the time (updated 36 times a day) and the date. Messages may be stored and retrieved for 96 hours. It also provides a host of additional information services, such as weather forecasts, sport scores, Dow-Jones closing figures, and lottery numbers, all for an affordable monthly fee of $12.50. That covers unlimited personal messaging and no additional start-up or service charges. Multiple-city-area service bumps the cost to $17.50 a month. The unit has only two buttons to handle all the available data. People who are unhappy with their cellular-phone bills now advise some callers to contact them on their Receptor lines.

In the future, The Receptor will make a great impact because of its ability to provide considerable information, especially when coded. Your spouse could send you, say, Code 17. To you this means, "The kids are ready to be picked up." You could tell ET to "call home." Phone numbers, coded or uncoded, are available, as are ski conditions and extensive information about stock-market pricing. All this is displayed in one tiny window, sized to fit your bank balance, which, by the way, can also be displayed.

The Receptor client base now numbers in the thousands. According to Seiko Telecommunication Systems, Inc., after they test larger cities like Seattle (a new service area that covers two million people), they intend to widen the system nationally and perhaps extend it into Canada. All of The Receptor's information is provided by Associated Press which is broadcast throughout Seattle via seven FM signals every two minutes. The Receptor captures the strongest, nearest signal, and shows that data when required.

Today, The Receptor offers only one-way functions. Tomorrow, it could provide two-way or three-way communications. In the near future, The Receptor will also offer more features, including traffic conditions. The Receptor carries a one-year warranty and sells for about U.S. $200.

No doubt there will be a Receptor in your future.

No Privacy

For centuries, governments have been controlling information. Now they aren't, or more correctly, they can't, and they are panicking. Don't worry about what you know, worry about what you don't know. Worry about the fact that analog cordless and cellular phones can be monitored, and that once cable is installed in your home, a novel could be written about its occupant, and that reading its first chapter, your friends would instantly recognize that it is all about you!

What do you know about geo-coding? For starters, it may reveal your exact global position by using your postal code. How? Geo-coding software instantly converts any postal code into longitude and latitude. Why is this important? Because *where* you live tells a lot about *how* you live. Until now, only the U.S. National Security Agency could take the next step. Now anyone can. The French provide a personal photographer for rent. Their company is called SPOT (Satellite Pour Observation de la Terre). A picture of your home can be taken from space and then delivered like a pizza, within the hour. Think about this. Anyone can commission the picture. And it only costs about a $100.

Do you have a mortgage on your house? Mortgages are just another commodity. Like soap or pork bellies, they are bought and sold around the world. When you apply for a mortgage, you don't get approval until you provide copious information and the lender has that information checked out. If the information isn't transportable, the value of the mortgage declines. That means one thing: the interest rate goes up. Because the rest of the world says they are not interested, you are at the whim of local lenders who also know the score and can charge higher rates, especially when your dollar is a depreciated currency.

My business card has my brain-scan printed on it in full color. It was shot by the PET (Positron Emission Tomography) scanner after I had ingested radioactive isotopes. The picture indicates what parts of your brain you think with. A different part of the brain lights up when you think work rather than play. But that's already old-fashioned. The newer QSI (Quantified Signal Imager) tells *what* you think. Today you need to wear a beanie on your head to make the device work, but pretty soon, with a stronger amplifier, anything will be possible. People still joke, "If you don't want it known, don't even think it." Not for much longer.

The knowledge pirate of today is the highwayman of tomorrow. This individual operates in tunnels of glass and isn't interested in money because you can only carry so much of that. The modern highwayman points a laser beam and says, "This is a stickup. Give me your ideas." Where does that put your privacy?

Any court order with geographic limitations in a globalized society, once translated into electronic or photonic form and accessed by the digirati, becomes unenforceable on *Homo informaticus.*

What does all this prove? Just as the industrial age gave us the haves and have-nots, the communications age has given us the knows and know-nots. The "knows" know how to access and disseminate information. They are able to keep constantly informed and act on the information they obtain. The "know-nots" don't even know what they don't know. This is creating a gap far wider and deeper than the division at an earlier time between the haves and have-nots. In the next millennium, information above all else will give people greater control of their lives.

The Knows versus the Know-Nots

The Knows	The Know-Nots
Ageless	Antiquated
Adventurous	Afraid
Curious	Uninterested
Creative	Complaining
Constantly changing	Remaining static
Learning daily	Stopped learning
Exhilarated	Exhausted
Excited	Worried
Computer literate	Computer illiterate
Increasing income	Decreasing income
Rising socially	Falling socially
Globally aware	Parameters limited
Highly mobile	Stuck in rut
Technologically aware	Technologically impotent
Investing in technology	Spending on vices
Surfing the Internet	Sleeping through opportunity
Constantly pushing the envelope	Retreating into the fortress

4 The New Order

Who's in Control?

In the next millennium, technologies, not governments, will make the laws and break the laws. Today, bureaucrats are still busily drafting and trying to enforce a slew of rules and regulations. Soon they will be acting in vain. With accelerating technologies, broadcast regulatory commissions such as the Canadian Radio and Telecommunications Commission (CRTC) will lose significant control.

In the near future, a new $100 million satellite uplink facility, recently developed by DirecTV Inc. of Los Angeles, will bring direct-broadcast satellite service to North Americans. The services *could* be received in Canada, but according to the CRTC they would be unauthorized.

Soon, however, the term "unauthorized" will be meaningless. In the near future, the Integrated Services Digital Network (ISDN) phone lines will be widespread. (The ISDN is already available in some locations.) With ISDN technology, it is possible to speedily deliver video movies over common telephone lines using new digital-compression techniques. What you can't get from the heavens (because of CRTC restrictions) you can already sneak in via phone lines. Point Roberts, Washington, is located 10 kilometers south of Vancouver International Airport. A video sent over the phone line from Point Roberts to Vancouver would cost 18 cents a minute to transport; that's about $16 (Cdn.) for a 90-minute movie. And that's for today's rate—watch American entrepreneurs cut that cost by at least two-thirds. American telemarketers currently pay around 13 cents a minute for calls anywhere in the United States, including Hawaii, Alaska, and Puerto Rico.

Telephone rates are falling worldwide. In Canada, the provincial phone monopolies are advertising rates that are 50 percent less than they once were. Prices will drop even more. And with fiber-optic links, it will soon be possible to zap a 90-minute movie to your home computer in a minute and a half. When movies arrive over phone lines, what will governments do? Will all phone lines be monitored? In Canada, regulatory action is necessary because Canadian monopolists cannot compete on a level playing field with more entrepreneurial American operators.

In Germany, a 14-inch-square satellite television dish

is currently in commercial use. Its resolution is excellent, far better than anything available in North America. What next? If in a couple of years dishes can drop from a diameter of 10 feet (120 inches) to 14 inches, or about one-tenth the size, will government regulatory bodies be able to keep track of five-inch dishes? In the works is a new radio-network satellite that will rocket skyward. It will offer subscribers 120 radio channels. The dish to receive its signals will be the size of a business card. Miniaturization will create a multitude of regulation-enforcement problems for the CRTC. As technology advances, governments will have less and less control.

Power Shifts and the New Revolutionaries

As change continues to accelerate at an unprecedented rate, governments are failing. They are unable to protect citizens at home and abroad from terrorism, stop wild fluctuations in currency, culture, and the environment, or even prevent illegal immigration.

Does the United States government really control south-central Los Angeles, Harlem, or the Bronx? No. Does Russia control Chechnya? No. Did the former mayor of Vancouver control his city? Not while union members were dumping their garbage on the steps of city hall to get a point across, then having the mayor pay them triple-time to remove it. Trying to fathom today's complex economic, social, and psychological order is an exercise in futility. Basically, there is one simple fact: the old order is collapsing.

When the Soviet Union was holding sway in the East, it balanced the power of the United States in the West. The disappearance of the USSR created an imbalance, and the teeter-totter went out of control. Other forces came into play, which are now trying to establish a new social order.

These changes appear chaotic. But beneath what appears to be uncontrollable is an elegant order. It is all happening in the effort to realign balances. Chaos is the most creative environment possible. Once you see the "order" in it, a new picture comes into focus.

As major military conflicts abate, violent events occur in smaller, individual arenas. Riots replace military battles. Defense shifts from the national realm to the personal arena. As people realize that the old order—big government, big unions, and big business—can no longer do what they were set up to do, everyone demands change. People may not know what changes they want, but they do know that the old ways are no longer viable or acceptable.

During the agricultural age, people who were rich had farms. Land produced food that could always be sold. But if a despotic government massively increased taxes, citizens were bound to the land and couldn't move away.

In the industrial age, owning machines was a means to acquire wealth. One cotton-jenny or steam engine could yield a greater income than the labor of 100 workers. But again, governments could tax, seize, and sell with ease.

Today it is a different game. Governments can't tax excessively and take over the software or information businesses. There is no land to seize, no machines to confiscate. Today the real wealth is in your head. It can fly to another, more welcoming land at the speed of light. You follow as just another starving refugee, unnoticed among the millions until you pick up the (software) luggage that waits for you at a network colleague's computer terminal. Then bingo! You're rich again. Wealth has been redefined.

Ever since communications satellites appeared in the heavens, they have been dissolving the ties that have bound countries together in the past. When talented and energetic people move out of a province or a country because of excessive taxation, the state really learns the meaning of trouble. Power can shift its base of operations. Already this is happening for the first time in history. Countries now face new meanings of competition as lower taxes attract wealth producers to foreign shores.

Another power shift is taking place in the political realm: leaders can no longer lie to their constituents. In 1993, then Canadian prime minister Kim Campbell informed her country that it was a world power. Canada a world power with less than one-half of 1 percent of the world population! Why does this sound so pre-Copernican? Campbell was trying to generate patriotism and nationalism. But it was impossible. Why? Because we have entered the fading age of nationalism and voters know it! Politics will never be the same.

Today we learn hour by hour about other lands and cultures. The industrial age gave us the haves and have-nots. Now is the time for the knows and know-nots. Today a wide-awake "know" can access information faster than a government, and because the individual is not a corporation or a department, that person can do more with the information in a shorter period of time.

Will revolutionaries of the future march down Main Street demanding bread, as revolutionaries did in eighteenth-century France, or in the United States during the Dirty Thirties? No. In those days, the masses comprised essentially unarmed citizens. Contemporary Western masses have a new hand-held weapon: the computer. Now revolutionaries or radicals can rapidly gather, absorb, and disseminate information, and this can cause more havoc than bullets. Governments can't control the spread of information. And even if they could grab and hold on to it, they wouldn't know how to process the knowledge.

No Censorship in Cyberspace

Let me use a murder case as an unfortunate example of how governments are growing increasingly irrelevant.

In Ontario, Karla Homolka was arrested and tried for murder. A judge, handling the case of Ms. Homolka's former husband, Paul Bernardo, who was also tried for murder, placed a ban on publishing details of her case, conviction, and sentencing to prevent this information from having an adverse effect on Bernardo's trial.

If the judge had made such a decision ten years ago, no one would have questioned it. Courts could enforce such bans, and tough sentences could be handed out for court-order infractions under subsequent contempt-of-court rulings.

But that was before cyberspace.

Now, electronic tentacles, invisible to the uninitiated, can enter a courtroom, acquire details, jump with impunity across national boundaries by satellite, standard or cellular telephone lines, and release information that is restricted in one country to a neighboring nation that is unencumbered by the host country's set of laws. That restricted information can then return to the host country regardless of legal regulations.

The Karla Homolka case dramatically identified the new split between the knows and know-nots. The know-nots, returning to Ontario from the United States, were met at the border by members of the Royal Canadian

Mounted Police (RCMP) who searched them for copies (more than one) of any American publications that might carry banned-in-Canada details of the Homolka case.

If that was the fate of the know-nots, what was the destiny of the knows? Here's an answer. I contact a "know" who explained how he handled the Homolka court ban: "I checked into America On-Line (The popular American data base.). Then I switched into their News section. Inside the library, I selected the *Buffalo News* from dozens of U.S. electronic–version newspapers.(Buffalo lies south across Lake Ontario on the other side of the Canada-U.S. border.) I typed in 'KARLA,'and a selection of 23 stories popped onto my screen. I took my pick, obtained the full text, read it, and then went off-line. If I hadn't been so excited, I could have downloaded the data into my computer in just a few minutes, and then immediately signed off. It would have been a bit cheaper. Then I could have read the material later at my leisure from my own now-updated and better-informed data bank."

My caller's words set me thinking. In Canada, it's impossible to censor court data if the information is reported to another country because it can be accessed directly via computer networks. If necessary, the country and the specific source of the "illegal" information can be disguised so that the individual, city, and country of origin might remain forever unknown.

How can laws, regulations, and sanctions designed for the industrial age be enforced in the information age, faced with electronic transfers and the soon-to-arrive faster, more powerful, efficient, and capable world of photonics? They can't. The laws must be changed to fit the new environment, not the other way around. Yet lawyers, judges, and others in the court system were trained in the ways of precedent. This is alarming, since for some things there are no precedents.

Who among the legislators can think the unthinkable in a land with no precedents, no rules, no laws, and no familiar pathways to new solutions for old problems? Lawmakers are living in the valley of blind, unseeing strangers who believe nothing has changed and who assume they still control their land. They are reluctant to acknowledge that a strange new world is evolving and that they are no longer in control. On the brink of the next millennium, information-rich slaves are rapidly becoming monarchs.

Electronic Democracy

The next millennium will bring a new form of democracy. It's called direct democracy and it could reduce and eventually replace representative democracy by allowing voters to be in constant contact with their politicians.

Take Canada, for example. Public reaction to the

1992 referendum on the Charlottetown Accord was a sign that the winds of change are blowing across the country. Almost without exception, the leaders of all the major political parties supported the constitutional changes as outlined in the accord and urged the public to do the same in a national referendum.

Most of those in favor of the Charlottetown Accord had a financial stake in its outcome; if the accord passed, members of the elite would be able to keep their overpaid positions. Large amounts of money were poured into the debate by people on government payrolls. Still, the accord was defeated by a considerable majority. The referendum changed forever the nature of the two-party political system in Canada. That vote made the Canadian electorate wary of the Progressive Conservatives (read Republicans) and the Liberals (read Democrats). Both of these political parties, as well as the New Democrats (read Socialists), lost public respect.

Why did the electorate turn against their political parties? In part it's because voters are much better-informed today than ever before. They will not take seriously those old political spiels, where promises go unfilled and the elected follow their own biased agendas. Until politicians consider direct democracy, Canada is going to remain difficult to govern.

As long as Canada remains difficult to govern, change will be imminent because politicians will look for a more effective way to run the country. Once change takes place, it will lead to new regulations, rules, and practices.

It won't be the old game anymore with different players and uniforms; it will be an entirely new one.

Let's go back in history to find another dramatic example of political change. During the Reformation, Protestants introduced the revolutionary concept that everyone is equal in dealings with God. Protestants believed that in prayer one didn't require the intermediary of a minister or priest. But Catholics didn't buy the notion, which caused a great schism in the ranks of the once almost united faithful. Still, most of the Western world adopted tenets of Protestantism.

The time is right for a shift in politics similar to that shift in religion. The analogy is obvious. With current technology, there is no reason that citizens should not be able to communicate directly with federal leaders about political issues. Direct consultation would replace government officials who had been elected in the days of representative democracy. The magic of electronic communications makes direct democracy inevitable. Does this signal the dissolution of government as we know it? Unquestionably.

Lifestyle Costs

How expensive is a lifestyle? It depends on how much money you have and where you live.

In India, 30,000 rupees is worth about U.S. $1,000, but it has the purchasing power of as much as $30,000 in the United States, or about $42,000 in Canada. An income of 900,000 rupees, or U.S. $30,000, provides the same buying power as U.S. $600,000. A U.S. $30,000 annual income in India could easily cover the expense of running a mansion, employing six to ten servants, wearing elegant clothing, and hiring people to do all the work.

The value of most currencies changes faster than the weather, but the international exchange rate is not the sole criterion of value. The first questions a North American should ask when considering moving to another country: "What are its taxes? Are the taxes applied on world income, as in Canada and the United States, or on income earned in the host country alone?" Many countries allow income earned abroad to be imported tax-free! Taxes on income are paid only in the foreign country where the capital is earned. Another question is: "What investments can be purchased in the country?"

People who study the wild and highly variable currency markets say it is no secret that today's currency values are affected by more factors than ever before. Take immigration, for example. Once upon a time, workers from low-income countries strove to find work in more affluent nations. Not too long ago, that meant seeking employment in the West. Immigrants entered the Western workforce at the lowest level of menial labor and tried to work their way up. If they reached their goal in savings, many returned to their still-developing country to retire in relative luxury. But it doesn't work that way anymore. Prices "at home" are now so high, some can't afford to move back.

The worldwide flow of immigrants, now greater than ever in human history, will slow down when more countries reach an acceptable level of influence in the eyes of their residents. If you have been fortunate enough to achieve economic success in a Western country, it would be prudent to review your options. North Americans, especially Canadians, should wake up and smell their national debts. Canada's debt is the highest per capita in the industrialized world. Brazilians, who have been traditionally criticized for their national debt, pay only 20 cents per capita for every dollar a Canadian pays in debt payments. Why? There are almost 30 million Canadians, but there are more than 150 million Brazilians.

Governments spend huge sums to attract the right kind of immigrants—those with special skills, entrepreneurial abilities, knowledge of local languages, and capital. Soon, however, it won't be enough for governments to concentrate exclusively on attracting "inflow." National governments will have to start making offers to retain those already within their country to compete with other more progressive domains, aware that economic stature no longer rests on physical natural resources but on the type of people who create wealth.

Few adults are adventurous by nature, but each age has its pioneers. Up to this stage in the development of Homo sapiens, acquisition of new knowledge and experience was of interest to few. But this is changing and incentives are being offered to people who possess unique skills and have knowledge in innovative, developing fields. Such individuals are prized by governments. Automatic citizenship and low tax rates are privileges that once went only with royalty. In the future, however, they may be reserved for those who visibly help to build a country.

Rebirth of the City-State

City-states, which were powerful from classical times through the Renaissance, are about to make a dramatic comeback in the communications age. Over the last 25 years, a subtle but distinctive psychological change has occurred in several dynamic cities in the West. Its cities have developed a vision that encourages citizens to "think locally, operate globally." In the next millennium, expect new maps drawn to reflect different economic, political, or visionary environments. There will be new regions of power — each with its own views, designs, and ambitions.

In the past, when asked on my world travels, "Where are you from?" I replied, "Canada." Now I say, "Vancouver." Why? Because today, Vancouver, one of the fastest-growing cities in North America, carries a better image than Canada.

Let me give you some American examples of the city-state phenomenon. Hollywood has had a long run for its money as the world's leading moviemaker. But now that the movie industry is being overtaken by computer enter-tainment, electronic media, and virtual reality, future city-states — including Phoenix, San Francisco, Orlando, and Seattle — where this technology is produced have more allure than Hollywood. And California's Silicon Valley, which comprises San Jose and a dozen nearby municipalities, now holds as much power — if not more — than any other city in the state.

City-states have sprung from metropolises disillu-sioned with large, faceless, bureaucratic governments focused on retaining power regardless of the effect on the country. Thriving, dynamic cities have chosen to ignore big government as much as possible. If you control the wealth, you sign the check and control the spending. Little wealth is created by federal, provincial, or state governments. Cities now produce the majority of the wealth, and with fewer people than ever before.

In Europe, Barcelona is called "the publishing heart of Spain." It is a city of six million that has created an industrial production of $63 billion a year. When this occurs, it's natural for some of the city's leaders to pop up and inquire, "Why aren't we our own country?" Even the language of Barcelona is different from that of the rest of Spain. It's Catalan, not Castilian.

Barcelona is not the only example of concentrated productive power in Europe. In the mountainous Rhône-Alps area, the 5.2 million French citizens of Lyons have increased industrial production to $90 billion. Even "industrial" doesn't mean what it once meant. Lyons is now the heart of production and development for French technology and software. Milan, the leading dynamic city in the Italian region of Lombardy, is the home of Ferrari, Fiat, and Italian haute couture. With just eight million people, Milan does $118 billion worth of business a year, while the rest of the country remains in relatively static decay. North of Milan and Lyons lies Stuttgart; with 5.6 million people, the German city generates $222 billion of wealth annually.

Such "poles of prosperity" have a magnetic effect. The young, the movers, the shakers, and the wealth creators arrive in these cities with new ideas, energy, and confidence. On the streets of Vancouver people seem to walk faster than in other parts of Canada. They also seem to think and act faster. The result remains to be seen, but it is a trend not easily diverted. Look for a hundred city-states, or whatever they may eventually call themselves, to appear during the next few decades. They want to move by themselves, create what they can, control what they earn, and what they spend.

Robot Warriors

War damages all parties involved, usually puts the loser out of business for some time, prevents the creation of wealth, damages the conquered territory, and presents even the victor with high repair bills. There had to be a better way, and now there is one. Today, factory robots can be remotely controlled from another room, from across the city, from the other end of the country, or from the other side of the world. Move the technologies of factories to combat zones and tomorrow's wars may be fought by robots controlled from a distant locale.

Full robot military parades may not be here tomorrow, but they will appear eventually. Military budgets have been cut, but once the robots are programmed and in place, all you need are batteries. And it is easier to obtain one-time procurement funding than subsidies for human programs that seem to go on forever. Politically and economically, the robot route is far more palatable.

Obviously, the robot soldier will not look like your typical G.I., but consider the potential effectiveness of a robot soldier built like a large metal ball. Try to think of the robot as a basketball converted into a turtle. When rolling downhill, everything gets tucked tight inside. When it comes to a halt, appendages extrude, eyes appear, antennae flip out, and regardless of the terrain (jungle, tundra, swamp), this soldier continues to be mobile.

In attack mode, the robot's velocity in a downhill roll could be considerable, a battering ram that only needs one shot and then goes into action once inside its target. Underwater robots could walk until the right sloping shore appears, always aware of location by means of a Global Position System. With wireless radio or infrared communication, such "soldierbots" could form and reform on demand, while constantly remaining in touch with command headquarters or aerial or naval cover. An almost projectile-proof exterior would cause small-arms fire to bounce harmlessly off the units' ball-like shield, the "soldierbots" still capable of returning mortar or bazooka fire while still mobile.

Privatization

If you think the cost of health care is high, if you think school taxes are skyrocketing, consider the amounts spent on providing public safety. The costs of police protection, penal institutions, health care, and fire departments have reached dizzying heights. What to do? Privatization may be the solution.

Arizona Rural-Metro, a company based in Scottsdale, Arizona, operates the fire department for that city and for 22 other locations in the Sun Belt. The company first caught my attention six years ago, when I heard about its privatization of fire-fighting services and its spirit of innovation.

Instead of fire engines, Rural-Metro runs its fire department using the classic Ford Thunderbird. The rear of the car is designed as a flatbed half-ton truck to carry fire-fighting equipment to any location. The high speed of the modified vehicle enables it to get to a site faster than large, lumbering old-fashioned fire trucks. Hence, Rural-Metro puts out small fires before they become formidable.

Today, Rural-Metro has expanded and it now provides paramedical services at many locations. When company sales reached $62 million annually, it went public. It's an understatement to say that Rural-Metro is operating in a brand-new environment. Fire protection, ambulance service, police protection, and criminal-custody industries are not usually open to the private sector.

In the last 20 years, the costs of operating fire-fighting and paramedical services have increased sixfold. The costs of police services has increased sevenfold. Keeping a cap on such soaring expenses seems all but impossible in the public sector. Therefore, the field is opening up to such cost-efficient pioneers as Rural-Metro.

Garbage collection was the first area to be tackled by the private sector, and substantial gains were made almost immediately. Today, wherever private companies handle garbage collection, more work is done. No longer do you see three municipal employees talking while the fourth tosses one green garbage bag after another into a waiting truck. Such inefficiency cannot be sustained, especially when both property and municipal taxes are rising faster than the ability of property owners to pay them.

The cost of operating correctional institutions has leaped by a factor of 15. And these increases don't even include pension obligations or, in the words of *The Wall Street Journal*, "the outrageous disability-retirement settlements that are now routine in these fields." Privatization of correctional facilities is a potentially huge market, but so far, according to Charles Taylor of the University of Florida, the private sector provides only 30,000 beds for a total of 1.4 million adult inmates. However, that is about to change. In minimum security, as in the juvenile system, the share is higher, up to 40 percent of 100,000 inmate beds are being run by non-government services. Even some inmates on parole are being supervised by nongovernmental operations. In Florida, some are monitored by the Salvation Army.

The jails are full, costs are running rampant, and the funds required to operate in an obsolete, inefficient manner simply cannot be sustained. The worldwide search for alternatives will produce more privatization in areas that were previously the domain of the public sector. Look at what is being accomplished by the Management & Training Corp. of Ogden, Utah. M&T is handling Job Corps centers for the U.S. government, and it has received another contract to run a "secure facility" in the California desert for several hundred parole violators. It also operates an Arizona treatment center for 450 drunk drivers and people convicted of narcotics offenses.

In most cases, privatization appears to provide cost reductions of between 10 and 15 percent. This has been accomplished by a thinner administrative staff, less red tape, and lower pension costs. Wage levels between private and public operations are not much different. The big difference is that private companies insist on the sort of financial discipline that the public sector has only recently begun to adopt.

Future Smarts

The first really big change in communications occurred in the second century shortly after the birth of Christ, when professional scribes and illuminators began decorating pages of writings with illustrations to make their work more attractive. From the seventh century well into the thirteenth, the Church dominated this type of "illuminated" communication. By the fourteenth century, scribes and artists, working with book dealers and wealthy patrons, took over the practice from the Church. In the fifteenth century, this art form faded because of the invention of movable type. Printed books with engraved illustrations replaced the work that had been created by long-laboring, church-enslaved monks working in lonely monastic scriptoria. Intelligence moved to the printed page and gave the Western world a far more efficient way to save, store, and pass on knowledge to future generations. The average citizen gained access to intelligence that had previously been the privilege of the high clergy and the wealthy.

Soon the Gutenberg-print format was being used around the world. Books allowed educational institutions to grow rapidly, spread in size and investment, and lay the foundations for the present system of controlling credentials. Today, in North America alone, more than half a trillion dollars (U.S. $500 billion) is spent every year on so-called education. That's more than three times the amount of money produced by the computer industry!

But the computer industry has done more than just grow rapidly. It is changing the meaning of intelligence, just as Johannes Gutenberg did 500 years ago when his printing press initiated the demise of church-and-state control of information.

The British magazine *The Economist* noted how the

computer industry can affect the world of learning: "In 1987, a budding classicist from the University of Lausanne, Switzerland, finished four years of academic labour. She had spent them scouring ancient Greek tomes for the sources of 2,000 anonymous fragments of medieval text." This student had been following the traditional, but now impractical, method of acquiring "intelligence."

As she was about to write her doctoral dissertation and finally quote her 600 sources, a new mode of research made her academic method obsolete: the data base, known as Thesaurus Linguae Gracae. It contained everything the student had found during her years of painstaking research—all the references she had amassed, as well as 50 percent more that she had missed. It contained every extant word of ancient-Greek literature—66 million words produced by 3,000 authors. All this information was now accessible and printable from a compact disk that cost $300.

Compare that cost to attending a university for roughly $25,000 a year for four years. That's $100,000. How does that compare to one month of intensive learning or three months of part-time study from a CD-ROM? When cost comparisons differ by 50 to one, change is rapid.

It is not only in ancient Greek literature that this new efficient manner of acquiring "intelligence" is changing the world and making established academic practices obsolete; it also applies to almost all the humanistic and physical sciences. The recently issued English Poetry Full

Text Database includes the texts of 4,500 volumes of verse. Dozens of other such electronic publications are available, and still others will soon come on the scene, making the knowledge of all disciplines, the basis of human knowledge, available to everyone, not just to the credentialed few.

As *The Economist* concluded, "Texts will be freed from academia's grip, just as books before them were freed by printing from the church and the wealthy . . . Some degree of conformity may be the price paid for new forms of access. The passing of the illuminated manuscript made the world a slightly poorer place; the coming of print made it a far, far richer one."

The vast sources of intelligence that are now available for a pittance will make our future a far richer one.

New Rules

In its present form, Canada's health-care system cannot continue to exist without soon collapsing. Medicare and private health-insurance systems will either evolve or end in chaos. The good news (to some) is that the route to change is already apparent. Some modifications are already on the books.

Once upon a time, you could ignore seatbelts. Not

any longer. If you get into an accident and receive damage or injury, if you were not wearing a safety belt, even the innocent party will receive only half the compensation. Insurance companies claim that ignoring the safety device contributes to the damage; they compare it to bailing out of an airplane without a parachute. The Insurance Corporation of British Columbia has issued a directive (now being tested in the courts) that states if your car sustains minimal or no damage (when hit from behind), you cannot claim for whiplash.

Future policy changes will reduce other coverage. For example, if you require kidney filtration for cirrhosis of the liver and have a record as a heavy drinker, you will have trouble collecting. The new rules will probably begin with smokers. Each year, smoking contributes between $300 and $900 million to hospital costs and related services in every province. That covers cases of cancer and emphysema. Soon, that crossed circle superimposed over a cigarette—the No Smoking sign—may appear on Medicare forms. Those people whose forms have a smoking sign will have to pay to use the system; nonsmokers will use it gratis or for a much lesser charge. People addicted to caffeine may also find another crossed circle on their forms.

It should come as no surprise that one day exercise may be compulsory. Statistics show that North Americans have become far too sedentary. Most of today's kids have been watching television steadily since they were born. Not much exercise there, especially with remote channel-changers. Adults and children should work out regularly. Lifestyles will change when this problem reaches its critical mass. Today you have to carry a driver's license. Have you considered a maximum-weight card that subjects the bearer to periodic inspections?

If you think that is far out, consider the following: the Alberta Medical Association is currently running full-page advertisements that point out, pictorially, the advantages of keeping fit. And for over a decade, the Canadian federal government has been running television commercials for exercise to encourage "ParticipACTION."

5 All Around the World

Eastern Attitudes

Not long ago, the *International Herald Tribune* published a revealing report by Tommy Koh, director of policy studies for the Singapore government. For 13 years Koh served as Singapore's high commissioner to Canada, then for six years he was Singapore's ambassador to the United States. He held similar posts in Mexico and at the United Nations. Koh's diplomatic perch provided him with a unique opportunity to study Western civilization and economics.

Koh's report points out something Westerners forget at their peril. There are alternatives to how we live. Koh reminds us of many features of the East Asian way of life that are at odds with the Western lifestyle:

• East Asians believe that every individual is important, but they do not believe in our extreme form of individualism. They believe every member of society is an integral part of a nuclear and extended family, clan, neighborhood, community, and state. Whatever East Asians do or say, it must maintain a balance between the individual and his or her society.

• Strong family ties are important in Asia. Divorce rates are lower in the East and the abandonment of aged parents is rare. The family is the building block, the foundation of society.

• In Asia, education is given top priority. It is taken seriously not just by the elite but by everyone. Parents take an active role in their childrens' education and act as teaching assistants.

• Singaporeans save 46 percent of their gross income annually (based on gross national product). This represents the highest reported savings rate in the world. The citizens and government of Singapore generally live within their means. Freedom from debt provides freedom to move.

• In Asia, the willingness to engage in hard work is viewed as a virtue. As a result, Asia is outcompeting Europe.

• Almost every country in East Asia is one big team. Unions and employers consider each other partners. Employees work cooperatively to form a national consensus.

• In Asia, governments maintain law and order and fill citizens' needs for jobs, housing, education, and health care. Citizens are expected to be law-abiding, to work hard, to save, and to motivate children to stand on their own two feet. Most Asian governments offer no unemployment benefits because they don't want to contract the welfare disease that plagues the West.

• More than 90 percent of Singapore's citizens own their homes. Singaporeans have the world's highest incidence of share ownership — over 300 percent higher than in Britain and 400 percent higher than in the United States. Annual bonuses in both the public and private sectors run around 25 percent of a worker's salary.

• East Asians value their way of life and are content with their living conditions. They feel that the West, with its pornography, obscenity, lewd behavior, and violence, *doesn't* have all the answers. Tokyo and Singapore are two of the world's safest cities.

• The free press is valued in East Asia, but not as an absolute right. The press must act responsibly and must not create tension among racial, linguistic, or religious groups.

Tommy Koh offers us a glimpse of the Eastern way of life as well as an insight into how Asians view our customs. For most of this century, North Americans have led the world in economic stability, standards of living, and medical, technological, and social advancement. Will we be able to continue to lead the world in these ways? Where will Western civilization be in 2020, just 25 years in the future? East Asia has learned a lot from the West. I believe it is time we start to learn from the East.

Asian Riches

Here's a riddle:

Q. Why did the man from Hong Kong cross the road as soon as he arrived in Vancouver?

Before answering the riddle, consider the following facts.

Ten years ago, a full 50 percent of the employment opportunities in Hong Kong were in manufacturing. These jobs have since been converted into service-sector opportunities. Ten years ago I predicted that by 2001, 80 percent of all jobs in Hong Kong would be in the service sector. Guess what? It has already happened, five years ahead of schedule.

On my trips to Japan in 1983, 1984, and 1985, I became enlightened. I met one of the largest makers of wooden shoes in Japan. Wooden shoes might sound like a Dutch invention, but they are worn by Japan's then peasant farmers in the rice fields. They are more comfortable and practical than sandals made of leather, fabric, or plastic.

When I visited Japan in the late eighties, there were

no longer thousands of farm workers wearing large straw hats, bending over to plant rice in wet fields. They had been replaced by small tractors with robot hands that planted rows of tiny rice plants underwater. The machines, which handled vast acreages, were driven by men wearing bright, Hawaiian-style short-sleeve shirts. I asked one of the men, "Whatever happened to that famous maker of wooden shoes when all his customers vanished?" He responded, "Oh, that man is far more famous now. He's the third-largest producer of computer chips in the country."

Later we ran into the computer-chip manufacturer. My interpreter passed on my query. "The Westerner wants to know how you moved so quickly from wooden shoes to computer chips."

Back came his reply: "I made quality shoes. Now I make quality chips."

I thanked him, bowed humbly, and walked away. I know my superior when I meet him.

In Hong Kong, there is no unemployment insurance. There is also no unemployment. When I was there a decade ago, this was the newspaper headline of the day: Industry Requires Another 22,000 Workers.

Last year, one weekend edition of the *South China Morning Post* carried 122 *pages* of "Employment Opportunities." The paper's headline announced: Jobless Rate to Rise in Rich Nations. But this headline was not really news in Hong Kong. Growth like this has been going on for 20 years. Some 50,000 Canadians have heeded the call and settled there, some for good, some for the good times.

Why do Canadians and other North Americans yearn for this foreign culture? The answer is success. An unemployment rate of 2 percent is not unemployment, since more than 2 percent of a country's workers are moving from job to job in any booming economy. Singapore, now fully developed, lists a 2.5 percent unemployment rate. Tiny Taiwan, with the richest currency reserves in the world (more than U.S. $120 billion), boasts only 1.4 percent unemployment, and South Korea is just about ready to go big time at 2.8 percent. But these unemployment rates are nothing new. Singapore, Taiwan, and South Korea have had virtually full employment rates for years. It's all attitude. Many people have two full-time jobs. Why? Because in some of these countries it's possible to make a million dollars a year and pay only 15.5 percent income tax.

In Japan, welfare is not necessary because there is no unemployment. Singapore and Taiwan have their versions of what some might call a welfare state, but we wouldn't recognize them as such because there are few handouts and no rewards for the unemployed. The only available government assistance is aid in the provision of housing— but not to rent, only to buy. In Singapore and Taiwan, they say even the lowest income-earner can save enough to own a house. But to do so, they have to do without something else. They have to change their priorities.

I'm a fan of the Singapore Central Provident Fund. By official edict, 18.5 percent of the country's total income goes into this pot. Employers top it up with even higher contributions. This is no 50-percent, Western-style tax. The money belongs to those who have invested in the fund and the government pays the interest. A relatively new feature allows a certain portion of the fund to be invested in Singapore stocks, bonds, and real estate. A Singaporean retiring today, after 25 years of work (unless he lost in stock investment, which is rare when everything has been growing at around 10 percent a year for 20 years), may retire with the equivalent of $1 million Canadian in savings (or in stocks, bonds, or property). Millionaires can look after their own retirement.

Now, back to the riddle.

Q. Why did the man from Hong Kong cross that road as soon as he arrived in Vancouver?

A. To buy the other side, silly. He did it with money saved, because his maximum income tax rarely exceeds 15 percent. He earns the same amount as the average Canadian. He bought the street while the average Canadian was busy paying taxes.

Singapore Success

More Canadian companies have offices in Singapore than anywhere else in Southeast Asia. Those Canadian companies—75 in total—are the smart ones. They are looking into the present and seeing our future. Singapore might be called the City of the Lion, but it sure doesn't roar. It doesn't have to. Its three million people have a unique and subdued manner. Their way of doing things is the envy of the world.

Despite the fact that Singapore is a fraction of Canada's geographic size and population, Singapore's economy is better-run and its manufacturing is of a higher quality. Singapore, second only to Japan in Asian per capita income, has no unemployment. Canada's debt exceeds $600 billion (the part you can see.) Singapore's is nil. Canada's actual per capita debt hovers around $25,000. Singapore shows a huge surplus.

Singapore's new nickname is "The Educated Island." Inflation on this brainy outpost just north of the equator is 2.4 percent. Foreign reserves total $40 billion, the highest amount per capita in the world. In the last few years, Singapore's economic growth rate was 10.1 percent—a rate that the country has sustained for more than three decades.

Singapore has the lowest birthrate increase in Southeast Asia. Education is not compulsory, yet almost everybody wants to go to school. The country's real literacy rate is

87.2 percent, but the population is not merely literate in the old sense. It is also computer literate. Ten years ago, Singapore's unions made computers available on a loan basis to anyone who was interested in using one.

Today, Singapore's gross domestic product (GDP) is U.S. $17,927 per capita; the country's dollar remains on par with that of the United States. Wages in Singapore are increasing by about 6 percent a year. But even that doesn't tell the whole story. More than 90 percent of residents own their own homes. Fifty percent of Singapore's population take a foreign holiday every year. Singapore's harbor handles 223 oceangoing ships a day, making it the world's most active seaport in tonnage.

By law, 20 percent of a Singaporean's gross income, matched by the employer's contribution, is deposited in a savings account; withdrawals are restricted to purchasing a home, education, medical care, approved stock purchase, and retirement needs. Consequently, the average Singaporean retiring today at 55 years of age has saved U.S. $753,000. He or she is a millionaire in Canadian dollars.

Income taxes in Singapore have dropped half a dozen times since 1974, while Canadians continue to face the 50 percent tax bite. Today, the Singapore tax bite is only 19 percent and taxes hardly affect people with low incomes. Even the efficiency of Singaporean government offices is fabled. Its Customs and Excise Department has long been respected for its maximum, one-day processing time to handle the daily average of 20,000 import permits. The department now guarantees import clearance in one hour! Singapore has the best-rated airport in the world and the most profitable airline (not too long ago they ordered 52 new aircraft at a cost of $14.7 billion, so soon it will have the world's youngest fleet). Almost all these advances were made in the 30 years following Singapore's independence from Britain.

Citizens live contentedly in Singapore, where the crime rate is low and the standard of living is exceeded only by Japan's. While the rest of the world chats about cash cards, Singapore acts. In 1993, all Singaporeans were issued a cash card for purchases. By 1997, Singaporeans will use the card to cover road-user fees, activated from a card on their vehicles' windshields. Singapore Airlines will also incorporate the card for in-flight services, phone calls, shopping, and so forth.

How can North America possibly compete with the highly successful Singapore? Companies that receive cooperation from Singaporean government have an immense advantage. In Singapore, the bottom line glows!

Four Tigers, Seven Dragons, and Six Years in the Future

Six years ago, I made the following observation:

"During the 1,824 days from January 1, 1985, to December 31, 1989, the greatest explosion of technology in history occurred on the third planet from the sun. This technological explosion was not limited to Europe and North America, as were earlier technological developments such as those of the Industrial Revolution in England in the eighteenth century and in Western Europe in the nineteenth century. This technological explosion started in the Far East, first in Japan. Then it spread to the Four Tigers—Hong Kong, Singapore, Taiwan, and South Korea. These countries shocked and overwhelmed the world with their new wares, their upward economic mobility, and their technological prowess."

That was six years ago. Since then, the explosion has continued. Those Four Tigers have become Seven Dragons, as Indonesia, Malaysia, and Thailand joined the fold. Within a few years, these countries will conduct more business transactions with one another than with the United States. The Seven Dragons are quickly adopting the latest technology. They have assimilated technology transfer faster than any other country in the world. North America, with so much tied up in the status quo, with its traditional industrial-age equipment, is much slower to acquire the latest, vastly more efficient, new technology.

Behind the Seven Dragons lurk three countries: India, Sri Lanka, and China—they are all becoming forces to reckon with. Meanwhile, Taiwan, the most economically sound country in East Asia, has the world's largest reserve of foreign currency, U.S. $120 billion. It is reported that half of that treasure is in the form of gold, not dollars or yen.

Here's a prediction for what we'll see six years in the future:

We have seen Four Tigers turn into Seven Dragons. In 2001, there will be Ten Giants: Hong Kong, Singapore, Taiwan, South Korea, Indonesia, Malaysia, and Thailand will be joined by India, Sri Lanka, and China. Think about it this way: It took the United States 200 years to produce one million millionaires. China did it in the last three.

The Next Economic Boom

Yesterday's economic boom in Europe and North America has moved to the Near West, once known as the Far East.

India may not be in the economic spotlight right now, but it is on the heels of the Four Tigers and Seven Dragons as an economic powerhouse. India has a population approaching 900 million, and its middle class, some 250 million people, has recently emerged from the dusty villages of the past and is rapidly advancing up the social ladder. Slower to awake, but potentially even more overwhelming in economic terms are Sri Lanka, and China with its 1.2 billion population.

These numbers may seem threatening. China, Sri Lanka, and India alone have almost 40 percent of the world's population. All the rising economies of the East have learned well from their mentor, Japan. Some, like Singapore, traveled the route of Hong Kong and Taiwan, initially making low-priced tin toys (remember when the words "Made in Taiwan" was an American joke?), then cheap appliances, followed by today's sophisticated electronic products. Tomorrow, the new dragons will be ahead of the West in biotechnology and in other ways we have yet to comprehend.

Soon, these industrious countries will no longer need access to the markets of North America or Europe, which will diminish whatever economic and political clout the West may have had in the past. Unless the West moves more swiftly than it did during the past decade of economic decline, especially in Canada and the United States, we should fold our tents and silently steal away.

Most emerging countries have not heard of the concept of high taxes to pay for social safety nets. Instead, citizens focus on saving a huge amount of personal income. Japan's phenomenal economic success is partially due to a national commitment to personal savings; each working person saves 22 percent annually to retirement. Today, such savings rates are found in countries that are trying to match Japan's growth rate; citizens are supplying capital to invest in the infrastructure that provides continuing growth rates. People in emerging countries are studying more, putting in longer hours, working for less, and are more patient than people in the West who traditionally want a payoff at the end of the next quarter.

In the West, the longshoreman's union, whose members earn an annual income of $83,000, is once again demanding higher salaries for its members to move boxes from ship to shore. Eventually, the same pattern will emerge that wrote off the militant members of John L. Lewis's coal miners in the anthracite areas of Pennsylvania. When coal was king, hourly rates demanded by miners became so outrageous that new forces emerged, including the funding to produce an alternative to their labor, namely, the automated coal-mining machine.

To fill a need for low-cost labor, the East may eventually export their labor forces to the West. That is the good news. The bad news is that sooner than we expect, the North American labor force might be competing with robots made in the East. What's the moral of this story? We have to recognize that the boom has moved from the West to the East. Start thinking about how you can profit from Eastern practices to enrich your Western way of life.

New Europe

A world without borders was envisioned by the science-fiction writer Arthur C. Clarke. In 1945, he wrote about placing satellites in heavenly orbit over the equator at an altitude of exactly 22,300 miles. Not many years later, the Soviets acted on Clarke's idea. *Sputnik* was launched and the world changed. Why? Because satellites fail to recognize national boundaries.

A half century after Clarke prophesied a world without borders, it is starting to happen. National boundaries are evaporating in the electronic era. Historians may soon regard January 1, 1993, the day the European Community (EC) was created, as a monumental moment in the advancement of civilization.

I celebrated the arrival of the 1993 new year in Britain. A few days later, I crossed the channel and visited Germany and Spain, to check the mood on the continent. Wherever I went, I found enthusiasm for the newly created EC.

At midnight on New Year's Eve 1993, citizens of the 12-member countries of the European Community ignited hundreds of bonfires that burned from Eastern Europe to the Cornish coast and from the Spanish semi-tropical Canary Islands, off the Moroccan coast, to the frigid and frosty lands of northern Scandinavia. For the first time in history, 12 countries, which for centuries had fought numerous wars, merged into a borderless domain of 290 million humans.

In London, I observed that most of the shoppers crowding Oxford Street were not British, but visitors from the continent. They were busy buying English, Scotch, and Irish products, as well as imported items. They were joyfully taking advantage of the recent abolition of most duty classifications, previously required passports, work permits, and residency requirements.

Across the channel in Calais, crowds of British consumers had eagerly awaited the new year, when they were permitted to bring home up to 120 bottles of wine purchased in France at $2 or $3 a bottle. (In Britain, wine was still selling at three times those prices.) Similar generous allotments applied to cigarettes and tobacco. Duty regulations were so relaxed that all a consumer had to supply was proof that the purchases were for personal use.

The elimination of frustrating border regulations was the first step in the plan to create a massive trading bloc within Europe—regulations which, in an earlier era, limited the free flow of commerce between countries, all within reasonable driving distances of each other.

In the immediate future, all EC member countries will be competing strenuously for economic survival. One month after the formation of the EC, the Hoover Corporation decided to close down its vacuum-cleaner –manufacturing plant in Dijon, France, and move it to Scotland. Why? French labor regulations are so strict that Hoover was not permitted to change wage scales or implant flexible working conditions. Government and workers in Scotland are not so regulation-driven. About the same time, the Nestlé corporation announced that it was selling one of its chocolate factories in Scotland and moving some personnel to Newcastle, England. In turn, it moved its Newcastle operation to France, to the very same town, Dijon, which Hoover was vacating. Nestlé found that Dijon was the most profitable location for its organization. Apparently, turbulence and opportunity go hand-in-hand.

If the EC overcomes some of the continually rising problems that plague contemporary corporations, its overall economic clout will be considerable. The continent-wide attempt of the EC to increase the free flow of goods and services may enhance the competitive benefits of a common market. Britain has launched a drive against red tape, reviewing 7,000 regulations that restrict business activity, its aim to cut unnecessary rules and regulations, like the one described by the *Financial Post* as "a law that stipulates the distance between coat hooks in factory changing rooms."

While Europe is scrapping tariffs and red tape, Canada continues to enforce more interprovincial regulations that restrict free trade. In the next millennium, Canada will have to decide if it really needs all those customs officials strung out along the Canada–U.S. border. Consider the costs in real-estate holdings, salaries, infrastructure, and bureaucracy that Canada bears to police its borders. All of this so the Canadian government might charge a 7 percent duty on products that Canadians purchase in the United States.

North America used to be called the New World. Many Canadians, hampered by the regulations of a bygone era, are beginning to think they've been left behind. North America has become the Old World. For a sense of what things will be like in the New World, visit the European Community.

6 Biomatters

Human Reconstruction

Fire was the first major discovery that changed the way we lived, and it continues to be something we wouldn't want to do without. Fire changed the world. We learned to use it to cook and preserve our food. Fire kept wild animals at bay during long winter evenings and warmed our caves. We discovered that the points on wooden spears lasted longer and became harder with burning. Fire led us back to our homes and torches lit the way when we were delayed after the hunt.

Fire allowed us to clear the forests and to melt and mix metals we found in the soil. We used fire and smoke as long-distance signals to other friendly tribes. Tin and brass made good swords until we invented steel, hundreds of years later. Fire was the single best thing that happened in the millennia before recorded history. What could surpass that initial and wonderful discovery? There's only one answer: biotechnology.

Certain to become the most controversial subject surrounding the beginning of the third millennium, biotechnology will do more than fire in directing us to tomorrow. Like fire, it will light up a new world and lead us into jungles as unknown but as rewarding as the ones our ancient ancestors found.

With biotechnology we will become gods. With biotechnology we can develop new life-forms and extract or add genes. We can cut, splice, and meld to create chimera —organisms containing elements of two or more different insects, animals, plants or even humans. And it won't stop there.

Geneticists, since Gregor Mendel pioneered the field in 1866, have been saying that we can never cross from the human, animal, or insect world into the regime of plants. But today such rules no longer hold true. Genes, which allow the dancing night-firefly to glow, have already been transferred into tobacco plants, so tobacco will actually glow before being lit. The anti-freeze gene from the Atlantic flounder has been transferred into canola, a high-profit Canadian crop. Now the plants can withstand early frost, thus lengthening the growing season on the Canadian and Russian prairies. Anti-freeze genes are being spliced into tomato plants to offset the same early frost that once harmed canola. Would such a gene offer advantages to explorers, skiers, military personnel, and others living year-round in Arctic or Antarctic conditions? Imagine the sums that could be saved on heating bills! At some future date, you may have a relative who is part mouse. Human growth-hormone genes have already been inserted into mice. Can the reverse be far behind?

At seminars, I often show people images of my Chimera Zoo. See the geep: half sheep, half goat. Watch the chickquail, a chicken with the head of a quail. Is a balding Uncle Ralph with the mane of a lion next? So be it . . . if science permits and consumers demand flowing blond tresses.

Biotechnology is already a favorite field for new ventures. Legislation may restrain the more bizarre in ultrarestrictive North America or Europe, but will that hold back Singapore, when one major biotech breakthrough could push three million Singaporeans economically ahead of 30 million Canadians?

Look at gene splicing as an archival warehouse, similar to the video-storage vault at CNN. Imagine the historical shows, movies, and documentaries CNN founder Ted Turner could produce if he had the time to pick, shuffle, merge, and assemble material from that storehouse. The same is now possible with billions of human genes, and billions more from animals, insects, plants, and perhaps many more from yet-undiscovered organisms. Is the loss of diversity a threat? More likely the threat is an overabundance of living organisms. Two hundred new animals are in the stable awaiting approval right now!

Along with gene splicing, we may soon see a much more radical use of hormone treatments. In Canada, 60 percent of all milk comes from one province, Quebec. And its production there is still subsidized. Americans can't believe it; a lot of Canadians don't, either. But it's true. Bovine Growth Hormone, however, can increase milk production 10 to 20 percent. How long will Canada's subsidized quota system stand up to public and even international political pressure, when Canadians already pay almost twice the amount for milk as Americans?

Laws will fall by the hundreds as technology changes the world. Some see chaos. I see opportunity, more opportunity than our ancestors ever encountered.

The Adventure Gene

Some nights I stay awake and wonder about the "adventure" gene.

Ever since life began, people have been itching to take chances and live on the edge. Some of us are outright daredevils, some entrepreneurs, some inventors, a few explorers, others financial risk-takers. Why do such people leave the herd behind and pursue untrodden paths? There are scientists who say the environment is responsible for this behavior, or that these people are following a family tradition. Maybe it's individual human nature.

But what if it's genetic? Consider the implications. Someday, someone unraveling the genetic code may serendipitously encounter what makes people adventuresome. Imagine how society might profit. Governments are always on the lookout for individuals daring enough to fly military jets. Investors are nowhere without creative entrepreneurs, innovative products, and original services. When a new item, concept or practice catches on, industries are often created and entire populations may benefit.

It seems the world simply doesn't progress without risk-takers. But why are such daring types, male and female, so few in number? Maybe they're rare because historically most people who took risks lost. Wrestling saber-toothed tigers wasn't carried out at quite even odds. Food-gatherers who had to sample to survive sometimes didn't.

Foragers who turned into farmers during the agricultural age must have had what they thought were bright ideas about raising crops. The first agricultural adventurers didn't dwell on the possible lack of rain or early frost or their crops being pelted by hail. Despite possible dangers, a segment of past populations was persistent and daring enough to reach the agricultural age.

A glance at history suggests that some people who risked the most survived in large enough numbers to carry on. Think of the daring nature of early explorers. As they progressed in any direction, they ran into the new, the unexpected, the scary, the exhilarating, the cold, the hot, the wet, the dry, often the calamitous, and sometimes the profitable. Yet they continued as long as there was new land or new water in front of them. Many explorers didn't make it. From the beginning, humans have had to contend with dramatically changing climates, earthquakes, floods, volcanoes, and a host of other natural disasters. Yet, despite the odds, Homo sapiens have flourished. Is it because some among us have possessed an adventure gene?

If an adventure gene is discovered, imagine the implications for future genetic research and for society. Today, we are able to add or extract specific genetic material from the human genome. Imagine what will happen when friends and relatives start "redesigning" their basic personalities. One day soon we might all have an adventure gene.

Cyberbirth

What exactly does "natural" mean? Natural childbirth is a matter of perception. Economics, minimization of pain, equipment, facilities, and staff are factors that make childbirth "unnatural." But few would forgo these conveniences and some would call them natural. Our perceptions are always being altered. In the next millennium, we will have to reconsider once again how we define the terms "natural" and "unnatural."

With increased knowledge of the human genome, there will be new scientific, and harmless, means to deliver physically improved future citizens into a progressive society. We are at the dawn of the age that will find us creating our own successors. By the year 2035, human fetuses will grow with the addition of desirable genes and the elimination of defective genes. The delivery of the newborn human child outside the womb will be a regular occurrence.

Usually, a major trend is discerned 30 or 40 years before it develops into an advancement. This lead time allows the fires of opposition to burn out before the trend can become mainstream. An erosion of traditional sexual mores and values lends support to the idea that one day it will be acceptable to "design" our own successors. A few simple facts may change some conservative minds. Only a 2 percent difference separates human DNA from that of the chimpanzee. If this small difference can increase intellect so substantially, imagine what will happen with the next evolutionary step. It took aeons to change our genetic makeup because of the laws of natural selection. The next step in human development will occur in a single lifetime through a scientific process accelerated by the current explosion of knowledge.

Scientists can now culture human skin like algae or seaweed. Some transgenic or trans-species mice and pigs are already part animal, part human. Even some plants are transgenic hybrids. In the field of biotechnology, the future will bring test-tube babies which are already at a stage to be conceived, designed, and developed either inside or outside the womb.

It's already possible for a postmenopausal woman to give birth. Soon children will be designed who are far healthier than their parents ever were, and they will be scientifically conceived, genetically altered, disease-resistant, and specially nurtured for delivery from artificial wombs. Births will not take place exclusively in vitro in glass-type aquariums. Some in-vitro births will be combined with a sophisticated and designed membrane-like placenta similar to its biological counterpart.

Genetic engineering marks a new beginning in the history of humankind. Before future births are a reality, biotechnology will have to confront a number of obstacles. There will be a violent clash between traditionalists — who comprise most of today's population — and forward-looking geneticists. Such clashes are commonplace whenever science offers the human race something hitherto sacrosanct.

Today there is almost total opposition to the genetic engineering of human beings. Genetic experimenters have few friends. But such hostility will turn into surprising support. Opposition will collapse when a single event or a series of events changes people's beliefs and expectations. The domino effect will then take over. There was a time when condoms were never discussed in polite society; now they are displayed on drugstore counters and advertised on television. Medical science has identified 440 diseases that result from defective genes. Once the benefits of gene manipulation become better known and understood, the public will celebrate advances in this field.

Virtual Medicine

A reigning king rarely takes part in a medical experiment, especially when it is performed on him. Whether he knew it or not, King Hussein of Jordan did so.

In 1992, Hussein was admitted to the Mayo Clinic in Rochester, Minnesota, for cancer treatment. The treatment started a train of events that culminated when the clinic arranged for diagnostic and surgical consultation with the Amman Surgical Hospital in Amman, Jordan. The clinic will send advanced medical services from the midwestern United States to the Hashemite kingdom—by satellite.

In the future, a direct television satellite will link the Mayo Clinic with the Amman Surgical Hospital. The $18 million project, known as the Amman Diagnostics Center, will include a new hospital equipped to perform surgery in televideo consultations between the two hospitals.

Although Jordan already has some of the best facilities in

the Middle East, the Royal Medical Corps (a wing of the Jordanian Armed Forces) will be the first medical team in any Middle Eastern Arab country to perform a heart transplant. Mayo Clinic experts will deliver lectures via satellite to local doctors. Moreover, from time to time, they will physically visit the hospital in a teaching capacity.

The long-distance display of medical techniques via satellite and television is not new. In 1986, I watched a satellite transmission between two medical institutions—one in Germany, the other in Japan—arranged for the purpose of sharing new operating techniques. For some years, North American and European hospitals have been doing the same thing by way of more or less local networks.

The next time you have an operation, it may be videotaped or even televised and sent by satellite to a teaching hospital on the other side of the world.

Happy with Your Toothbrush?

Like most people, you probably put toothpaste on your toothbrush, scrub your teeth faithfully twice a day, and go the dentist twice a year—to spend $100 a pop to have your teeth cleaned. Now there is an alternative. The Soladey-2 is a Japanese toothbrush made by Shiken of Tokyo. It cleans without toothpaste, and is so effective that its users hardly ever have to go to the dentist.

Here's how it works. When brushing with the Soladey-2, keep your mouth open to the light. The key element in the brush is a titanium dioxide rod. When the rod is exposed to saliva and solar or artificial light, it creates a photonic reaction that produces negative ions. The negative ions attack the bad, positively charged hydrogen ions that are produced from the acid in plaque and tarter on teeth. The process neutralizes the acid and loosens the tarter, and the brushing cleans off what normally would continue to stick to tooth enamel. The toothbrush never vibrates, and there are no unpleasant tastes connected with the cleaning process.

The Soladey-2 lasts about a year before its brush begins to wear thin. Then one pulls gently on the brush section, while firmly holding on to the handle, and the unit separates. Replacement brush-heads, available for a reasonable cost, click into place, and the Soladey-2 user is okay for another year or two. The valuable titanium rod does not disintegrate, dissolve, or diminish in size. It simply serves as a catalyst, and it is lifetime-guaranteed.

2,000 Days as a Cyborg

In August 1989, I became a cyborg. I had a plastic lens surgically implanted in my right eye. Now I consider myself one of a new breed that is appearing within our species faster than many of us realize. The implications could be life-threatening: we may be creating our own successors.

Here is how it happened. Since the age of 12, I have been wearing glasses. In the last decade, my lenses were as thick as Coke bottles. Yet my vision didn't improve, even with the latest optical prescription. While driving at night, my right eye kept seeing every car headlight as a rising sun bouncing off the water.

An ophthalmologist in New Westminster, British Columbia, gave me a routine eye examination and told me to come back in a few months. My next visit took an hour, involved stronger eye drops, and led to a date for the implant operation. The procedure was less trouble than getting my teeth cleaned. It took 30 minutes and was painless with a local anesthetic. Thirty minutes after the operation, I was on the phone.

Within 48 hours, my vision was 20–30 (previously 20–300, white-cane country). After three months, it improved to 20–18. Now I see better with one eye than I ever saw with two eyes and glasses.

But the unexpected benefits are not only in what I now see. No longer burdened with poor eyesight, I stand straighter than I ever did. As my vision expanded, so did my mind. Shortly after my second eye operation, I recall flying a small plane over the California desert one very hot summer day and experiencing unlimited visibility. For the first time, I understood the meaning of that song "On a Clear Day You Can See Forever." Veins in a leaf now seem like my veins. Trees on distant mountain peaks now seem so distinct.

Now that I have repaired my eyesight, I wonder what else I might improve. A click on my computer tells me that there are currently 72 "off-the-shelf" body parts available. There are reference books available on this subject matter and all of them have interesting titles. One book is called *Borrowed Time* and it was written by A.L. Plough. Another, by G. Skurzynski, is called *Bionic Parts for People*. It seems I am not alone in being a cyborg.

In fact, there are now approximately six to fifteen million cyborgs in North America. Today, body parts can be replaced with various plastics, metals, and synthetic fibers. Artificial hips, knees, and other joints have been successfully implanted in persons whose natural joints were damaged by arthritic disease or accidents. Artificial heart valves and cardiac pacemakers have been implanted in many thousands who were afflicted by crippling heart disease. The artificial larynx or "voice box" is another well-known implant.

According to some scientists, in the dim and distant past, we came down from the trees. Some creatures stood upright, walked into the unknown, and became Homo sapiens. Other creatures climbed back into the safety and security of the trees and succeeded in staying as they were. Are we creating our successors? Are we beginning to evolve bionically?

I believe we are at the beginning of our bionic evolution. The next stage is close at hand.

7 Entertainment

Computer Synergy

Here's the pattern for tomorrow. I predict the demise of the telephone and television, which in turn will directly benefit computer technology. I like to call the telephone and television "pinnacle products." They are currently the tops. Their development has affected everyone, and they provided the opportunity for us to move from the old industrial age into the new communications age.

The problem with the telephone and television is that they operate on a restricted portion of the electromagnetic spectrum, or bandwidth, and they are so hobbled by regulatory bodies that their further development or diversifcation is next to impossible. Eventually, the regulatory bodies, which grew up in a garden of frequency scarcity, will wither and die along with their pampered and fragile flowers in tomorrow's brand-new, untethered, and unrestricted jungle of electronic and photonic freedom.

In the new age, restriction or scarcity of bandwidth will be virtually unknown. The new environment will allow a different set of flowers to sprout. These new species, like single-electron electronics, electron-spin transistors, three-dimensional and holographic memory devices, will give more power to self-contained, low-cost computer intelligence that has the power to change direction and frequency.

Most important, the world will see larger numbers of small computers produce the largest organization in history, the synergistic network. A billion computers, when linked together, will have, through the power of synergy, the dynamic to become stronger than ten billion individual unlinked computers. The desert wasteland of television will disappear as the lush jungle of diversity and communication flowers, flourishes, and completely overrides television and the telephone. As networks expand, the power and the possibilities of the synergistic network will dramatically increase for everyone. Computers will become increasingly interactive. Present-day television injects; the synergistic network will give and receive.

Tomorrow there will be anywhere from 500 to 10,000 television channels. But every one of tomorrow's computers will have a greater capability than the local television station of today. In the future, you will be able to use your computer to program your own show or series and to create your own personal electronic art. Eventually, a billion people will be on the Net as customers and suppliers! No matter how weird your product or service, among the millions of fellow Internet subscribers there will be 50,000 or so who will like your style. That's enough for a good business.

The computer world is constantly expanding and improving its mode of operation. It is moving from processing information in 32-bit mouthfuls to 64-bit mouthfuls. This doubling of capacity is significant. It is increasing—four billion times!—the capability of computers to access memory directly.

Computers hooked up to networks grew during the last five years from 10 percent of all extant computers to 60 percent in North America alone. Fifty million new computers will appear worldwide this year. The majority will eventually join the synergistic network. Within a few years, Internet will carry monochrome pictures at high speed, even color pictures. In time, the synergistic network will metamorphose into a single gargantuan processor. The computer infrastructure of tomorrow will do more for the communications age than the U.S. Interstate highway system did for rural America.

The Death of Celluloid

The motion picture industry was born more than 105 years ago when George Eastman came up with a ribbon of celluloid. Since then, movies produced on film have been duplicated in quantity, and these valuable "dreams" have been distributed around the world on reels housed in sturdy metal containers.

But the ways of the past are rapidly changing and the day of reckoning is coming for the motion picture industry. Pacific Bell (PacBell), the regional telephone company, has just signaled the death knell of the film industry. They have taken celluloid out of film technology. In conjunction with the Sony Corporation, they will shortly be beaming movies into a dozen theaters in the Los Angeles area. Transmissions via fiber optics to between 2,000 and 3,000 theaters nationwide will likely follow. Pictures will be high-definition. The old distribution system will no longer be economically viable.

Consider this: Eight trillion bits of data are contained in the average two-hour movie. The PacBell system digitally compresses this data by a factor of 25 to 1, into a mere 320 billion bits or 40 gigabytes—for rapid transmission with high definition. Financial savings to the American movie industry alone could be immense, as much as $300 million a year.

With beam technology, what will happen to the unionized projectionist? As with firemen on steam locomotives when diesel engines arrived, their days may be numbered. With this new system, it is possible that one person could program all 25,000 cinema screens in America from somewhere else in the world. No doubt one casualty will be the word "cinema." Some new term will be needed.

Too complicated you say? It will take decades to perfect? Not so. In 1993, while shooting *Schindler's List* in Poland, director Steven Spielberg found the time between takes to edit *Jurassic Park* via PacBell's ABVS (Advanced Broadcast Video Services). PacBell is well positioned to handle the "Cinema of the Future" because the company knows the needs of showbiz people, having serviced them for years. ABVS got PacBell deeply into digital transmission. Now they are ready with the technology for a wealth of new clients.

A $20 million movie has about $5 million allocated for distribution expenses. Soon these figures will be a part of the past. Packages of photons racing at the speed of light may be compared, relatively and economically speaking, to electrons speeding through the copper wires of Samuel Morse's now-obsolete invention, the telegraph, when it replaced the Pony Express.

Desktop Video and the New Hollywood

Just as desktop publishing has made substantial inroads into many forms of printing and publishing, desktop video will become one of the many new fields that will excite, engage, and entice people to move into "showbiz." Desktop video will likely grow larger than Hollywood and create countless new jobs. Let me explain.

In the early days of computing, we sought and continually found increasingly productive ways to do more with digits and letters. That was fine for the past, but today we are no longer dealing with the same rudimentary symbols. Now we are moving into a faster and more complex world of images. We need something to handle the multimedia mix of tomorrow. And lucky for us all, digital nonlinear editing has emerged to make the shuttling of images as simple as moving around digits and letters.

Pictures on computers require vast amounts of storage space. The same quantity of memory is needed to hold one picture as the text of a 300-page book. But the latest magnetic hard-disk drives and optical-storage devices now accommodate desired compact storage space. And digital editing is here to provide the software. As a result, it is possible, economically and photonically, for computers to offer high-quality broadcast resolution.

Software systems that once cost hundreds of thousands of dollars are now available on top-of-the-line home computers that are rapidly becoming as sophisticated as fully professional equipment. A few years ago, the special morphing effects of the movie *Terminator* cost an unprecedented amount. Now, the special-effects sofware which created many of the most memorable *Terminator* images, is packaged for the personal computer for as little as $99. Theoretically, today it is possible for anyone to make a full-length motion picture on a computer, at a fraction of previous film costs, including fancy graphics as seen in movies and on commercial television.

Images, music, voices, and sound effects can all be incorporated into movies efficiently and quickly and at a price that will not break the bank. Everything can now be done on the keyboard far faster than with the linear editing of the past. And it's all done in real time, with no picture or sound degradation when copies of disks or videotapes are produced.

Digital Film

Electronic cameras that require neither expensive film nor timely processing are not even a decade old, yet they are about to revolutionize an entire industry.

For almost five years, I have been experimenting with new electronic cameras. Not only do they operate without film, they are also lighter than the older-style cameras. And all a user has to do is point.

My first new camera was the Sony Still Video Hi-Band Format Mavica, Model MVC-A10, with a 15-mm f/2.8 lens. It shoots and records 50 fair-resolution color pictures on a small reusable Mavipak 2-inch-square video floppy disk. The same disk captures a 10-second sound-byte, each time the camera takes a picture. Now photos of a celebration on New Year's Eve capture not only the revelry but the sound effects.

Once pictures are taken, no film development is necessary. Plug the camera into a television set or computer to see what has just been recorded. The picture can be faxed around the world in seconds, or with another attachment, it can be printed out, Polaroid-fashion, or sent directly to a laser printer.

The camera's standard attachment device also charges its battery. There is a display window on the camera that shows what number picture is coming up, if the disk is protected against accidental erasures, and how many seconds remain for sound recordings or weak batteries. The unit has a built-in flash, shooting mode selector, a Macro or Micro chooser, and a 10-second delay self-timer. The camera weighs but one pound, six ounces, including battery pack.

The Mavica cost me $300. It's a bargain at that price. Since then, Sony has concentrated on a line of more sophisticated and more costly, high-resolution cameras. My latest camera is the Apple QuickTake 100 made jointly by Sony and Apple Computers. While the QuickTake takes only 32 pictures (only eight of which are in very high resolution) and costs U.S. $700, picture clarity is excellent. It has the equivalent of a floppy video disk built in on a chip. After taking and viewing the eight or 32 pictures, or any combination, one can dump them all into a computer hard-disk drive and then erase all those shots on the chip, point the camera, and start over.

Comic Books and Satellite Dishes

There are two industries in Japan that have not yet exported their products to the West. Both are money-making opportunities waiting to happen.

The first industry is in comic books, what the Japanese call the *manga* business. The Japanese are among the most literate people in the world, yet every subway newsstand and neighborhood bookstore displays hundreds of colorful comic books. These are not slim booklets, but 200- or 300-page books printed in full color. The majority of purchasers are adults. The Japanese feel no embarrassment if seen reading comics on the subway lines that crisscross Tokyo. Perhaps it's because their comic-book industry is worth $8 billion.

Forty percent of North Americans never read a newspaper. Some surveys show that 20 percent of North Americans are totally illiterate. Up to another 20 percent are functionally illiterate and cannot thoroughly understand a complicated book or document. Imagine the demand when someone comes up with the right comic book to grab this audience!

With only half the population of the United States, the Japanese spend seven times more on comics than Americans. If the highly literate Japanese buy that many comics, I see opportunities here. More and more of our high-school graduates can't read or write, but they understand images from television, the movies, and video. Why else are they watching MTV?

The opportunity lies in creating comic characters that will motivate North Americans to reach for a comic book the way they now reach for a Coke. Don't say I didn't point it out to you first! When you do develop a money-making comic book, send me a copy.

What's another potentially huge opportunity? Dishes, but the kind that rest in the sky. A few years ago, in the Japanese laboratory of Uniden, the world's largest man-ufacturer of cordless telephones and dozens of other high-tech products, I saw what they were doing with microwave frequencies in the 20/30, 60, and 90 GHz range. They knew that it was theoretically possible to bring in a picture on earth from a communications satel-lite at an altitude of 22,300 miles over the equator. Their goal then was to devise a dish the size of a saucer that could pick up a signal through a wooden roof! They might have succeeded by now. If not, why don't you try?

The Canadian Radio and Telecommunications Commission (CRTC) is making things easy. The federal regulatory agency ruled that Canadians can only watch direct-to-home satellite transmissions when they come from Canadian satellites. Their ruling supports the regional Canadian cable monopoly. At a time when everything is being deregulated, the CRTC still thinks it can set the rules.

The next big opportunity lies in the miniature satellite dish. Develop a satellite dish so small, it can be hidden almost anywhere, a dish so inconspicuous that the

Canadian "satdish police" will be unable to spot it.

If you can't come up with the miniature satellite dish within the next two years, forget it. The Yanks and the Asians are working on it now, and the odds are they will perfect it soon. If the new product comes from Hong Kong or Taiwan, it may look like a dog's water dish, but when you turn it over, it will serve just as well as a satellite dish. Technology marches on.

Play Pets

Robotic pets may be the way of the future. Meet the latest creature from Japan—Perky the robot angelfish.

Fish in aquariums demand attention. Their water must be kept warm and clean, they require daily feeding, and one must watch out for fish itch and other aquatic diseases. Now, however, all these worries belong in the past. The new age of Aquarius has arrived.

Perky the robot angelfish comes in his own small and attractive aquarium called Aqua-World, where the underwater acrobat swims, wiggles, dives, and loops. Perky is the only pet that is absolutely no trouble. He requires no food, leaves no mess, and performs on command.

Perky looks like a cross between an angelfish and an elaborate goldfish, and he is always friendly. Perky never gets lonely, so you can go away for months. When you come back, just flip Perky's activation switch and he's happily back in the swim of things.

Perky and his underwater world weigh less than a pound, including water, and he and his Aqua-World are portable and come complete with batteries. Perky is a low-overhead boarder, so costs are minimal. Simply replace his batteries about once a year (varying with how many miles you want Perky to swim and perform) and you have the ultimate apartment pet.

If a mechanical pet is not up your alley, what about a virtual one? Computer specialists Demetri Terzopoulos, Xiaoyaun Tu, and Radek Grzeszczuk, associated with the University of Toronto, have developed virtual fish, simulated mechanical denizens of the deep that function as if they were real. The team at the University of Toronto is trying to teach these virtual fish to be a superior species. What's next? Will virtual fish soon learn how to survive better? To hunt more expeditiously and eat more nutritiously? To swim more effectively? To reproduce more productively? To more thoroughly guard offspring against predators?

The Terzopoulos/Tu/Grzeszczuk virtual fish incorporate all known habits, physical characteristics, and attributes of real fish. If it looks like a fish, swims like a fish, and makes love like a fish, you are pretty safe in saying, "It ain't no turtle." Set up with feedback brains that "remember" what they did earlier, their fish appear to "improve" themselves. In a technical sense, these fish are "conscious." They contain sensors for emotional and physical conditions. They know darkness when it falls, sense other creatures nearby, detect temperature changes, and have been "taught" about sex and starvation.

If the virtual fish eventually acquire fertilization and spawning abilities, will they be able to reproduce? If an exchange of DNA information takes place in subsequent generations, will the species evolve? Can they duplicate a biological system in a more mechanical way? We went through the whole industrial age without even imagining such possibilities. Now we can.

High-Tech Dogs

Near Whitehorse in the Yukon Territory, dog-team breeders, trainers, and drivers are mushing into tomorrow in a far different way than yesteryear. Dog teams have found new life with technology. Dogsledding is speeding into a faster and more scientific race. Equestrians had better watch out!

From my southern perspective, it was hard to figure out why this lonely, cold, and distinctively macho challenge is moving into the big time. The basic reason is money. The Japanese are now flying into the Canadian North and learning how to handle, ride, and drive modern dog teams. They are doing it for personal satisfaction and delight, and also in an attempt to capture the large purses that dog-race promoters now offer.

An Alaskan or Canadian–trained professional dog team, including sled, food, and equipment for a major race, plus accommodation and training for the human driver operating close to or north of sixty, now commands a rental fee upwards of $40,000 for a two-week–long race.

My introduction to the sport was at the Kipisa Kennels, 45 kilometers north of Whitehorse. There, kennel owners Michael and Lillian Hyslop spent several hours explaining the dogsled racing world. For openers: Some dog-team races are long. The Alaskan Iditarod is a grueling 1,165 miles long. Yukon Quest is a bit shorter. Now there is a growing demand to make dog sledding an Olympic sport.

Along the trail, for those who manage to keep to it, there are veterinarians stationed at widely spaced intervals. Although no medical files accompany the dogs, there is no problem. The vets whip out a handy bar-code infrared pencil, pass it over the dog's ear or loose skin in the neck (which has an implanted microchip), and presto, the dog's medical history (birth date, age, diet routines, and so forth) appears on the computer screen.

The canines are small, about 45 to 50 pounds, compared to the 75 to 80 pounds of traditional huskies. They are mostly muscle; fat content is down to 20 percent from the 50 percent of yesteryear's dog teams. Modern harnesses are light, padded with polar fleece, and leave no sores or rub marks—the "brand" that nearly every sled dog once had to endure.

Although at first glance they appear ordinary, today's dogsleds are more efficient than ever. Practice runs often include a 60-second "pit stop" to turn a sled on its side to replace the thin PVC plastic quick-change runners, which fit into grooves on its bottom, with a set that is better suited to the day's snow conditions. After the new runners are in place, the sled is flipped upright and the race continues. Modern sleds are half the weight of those on the market only a few years older. The latest models are made of such low-weight, mixed-alloy materials as aluminum and titanium.

The real fun of dogsledding comes when you drive by yourself. Hot-rodding was never like this. When the driver takes his or her weight off the high-tech, high-alloy brake, a kind of woven metal rug with claws that dig into the snow, there's a sudden flurry of ice.

Michael Hyslop conducts a mini-training course of about 20 hours, which includes information about the history and principles of mushing, the evolution of the sport, suitability of various dogs, and the selection and use of equipment. It ends with a seminar on dog care conducted by veterinarian Jim Kenyon, who has extensive experience caring for sled dogs for both Whitehorse and Yukon Quest mushers. The course culminates with the thrill and enjoyment of driving a team "of your own."

Someday soon, teams of 18 dogs—tested for steroids and other drug use of course—might be running 3- to 20-mile sprint races, or 150- to 500-mile mid-distance races for Olympic gold.

8 Other Trends of Tomorrow

Practices

Granny Hackers and Long-term Care

It is no secret that the North American population is aging rapidly. And with the number of elderly people living longer than ever, long-term care could well be one of the best growth industries. Tomorrow's seniors, however, will be a new breed, the majority unwilling to enter long-term care facilities at the "young" age of 70 or 75. A number of changes will improve the quality of life of most Canadians, thereby keeping most of the older population out of long-term–care facilities until they are at least into their eighties.

At age 75, I am one of the active seventy-plus set. Every year, I fly more than 200,000 miles, present roughly 70 seminars, and travel to the world's most remote regions, from Africa's Rift Valley to Arthur C.

Clarke's patio in Sri Lanka. I am constantly on the go, seeking unusual technological installations and scientific developments. At my age, this kind of lifestyle would have been considered impossible as recently as the turn of this century.

Demographic and lifestyle trends demand that long-term–care facilities keep up with the latest technological innovations designed to aid the aged. The "new" elderly, more discerning than their predecessors, want the latest in creature comforts: healthier mattresses (perhaps with magnetic force fields) with built-in vibration controls, and state-of-the-art heating controls. They want bigger and better television sets with higher-resolution pictures. And the phenomenon of the "granny hacker" may turn some residents into surfers on the Internet.

Once addicted to the lively global stream of international Internet action, some residents of long-term–care facilities might find the attraction of ordinary television dimming. It is this change in access to information that will present the greatest challenge to long-term–care staff, as they will be asked technical questions that can stump even the semi-computer literate. The same feelings of inadequacy now prevalent in public schools, where students are often more qualified than teachers to handle computer transactions, could pervade the long-term–care sector, as residents have the time to hone their techniques and staff do not. Knowing that this advanced technology is available, tomorrow's elderly might base their residency decisions on the level of technology offered by a facility.

Such potential developments have another dimension. With such mind-active interests, residents might stay healthy longer. The phone will no longer be their only link to the outside world. At a relatively insignificant cost, they, too, will have the opportunity to "go global." And it's only a matter of time before virtual reality invades long-term–care facilities. Expending very little physical energy, residents will be able to do some astounding virtual traveling, which undoubtedly would keep seniors mentally active.

What about staff? Trends coming across my screens suggest that staff will be better educated and more energetic . . . to match their clientele. For owners and operators of such establishments, the financial investment will be considerably higher. The never-ending battle for adequate government funding based on a per-diem minimum will likely continue. Ongoing downsizing and the cost of accelerating technology will clearly demonstrate that the future — not only in long-term–care facilities — is capital, and not labor-intensive. This will provoke a big change in management and labor bargaining.

Institutions expressly designed for the industrial age will not survive in the fast-moving, changing environment of the communications age, no matter how much we might want to keep them around. Nostalgia has no place in the business of the future. That same bulldozer of change now rolling over our planet will invade even the formerly quiet inner sanctums of the long-term–care facility.

Home Office

Cities are experiencing sizable vacancy rates as a result of corporate downsizing. Worldwide, the vacancy rate for office space, as reported by local boards of trade and real estate organizations, is around 20 percent. The true figure is probably closer to 30 percent. Many large companies which once used three or four floors in an office complex now have an empty floor. This space is transparent. No one sees it, but the company is trying to sublet it.

Building owners want to rent their own empty space, not space that belongs to some responsible company they have on the hook for another ten or 20 years. Meanwhile, the company subleting is embarrassed that they don't need what their top executives once decided would be necessary for the next decade. Education and experience never taught yesterday's executives to prepare for surprises.

The new phenomenon of "teleworking," or working at home, is already changing the face of the modern urban center. Fewer and fewer people are traveling into cities to work in rapidly emptying office towers; they are staying at home, where their office has already been built. It was the den, or an extra room now converted to function as a far more productive space. No additional structural investment or rent is required. New work-at-home equipment (appliances for productivity) must be installed, but at minimal cost, since most of the necessary wires connecting them to the world of cyberspace are generally already in place.

There are a number of conspicuous advantages to tele-working. Rush-hour traffic declines as fewer people make their way downtown by subway, bus, or car, and less gas is used. That means less pollution, fewer accidents, and lower automobile-insurance premiums. Not only do transportation costs drop dramatically for the stay-at-home worker, but dry cleaning and clothing bills also diminish. Expensive restaurant lunches and day-care payments save a lot of cash when multiplied by 240 working days a year.

When the workplace is located in the living space, there is increased traffic from package-delivery or mail-order companies and less business for downtown office suppliers. This creates more empty space and reduces office rental rates, although still not enough to compete with work-at-home rents several magnitudes lower.

Outsourcing and Privatization

Years ago, I predicted that outsourcing and privatization would become two of the biggest trends of the 1990s. Today, these two practices are both starting to hit hard.

Electronic Data Service (EDS), American industrialist Ross Perot's old company, is one of the leaders in outsourcing. Over the past few years, EDS has acquired more than 7,000 clients, and the company now does $8 billion worth of business. It provides operations previously performed by the public sector at less cost, while still making a profit and paying taxes. On a smaller scale, maintenance and cleaning companies are springing up to undertake office cleaning and repair jobs, offering services to companies at a much lower cost than in-house staff.

Outsourced services offer competitive rates because they operate efficiently. Workers no longer sit around when a job is finished, putting in time until five o'clock. When one project is finished, the new private-sector companies move staff on to another job for another company in another building on another contract. Productivity flies over the moon.

Pacific Press which publishes two dailies, *The Vancouver Sun* and *The Province*, used to pay what some observers claimed were exorbitant wages to in-house truck drivers who delivered the morning paper and later that day the afternoon paper. Eventually, the dual deliveries had to come to an end because tracking costs became exorbitant.

Pacific Press sold their trucking division and the trucks. As part of the company's new marketing strategy, the afternoon paper, the *Sun*, became a morning paper. In a classic example of outsourcing, the outfit that purchased the trucks agreed to deliver both papers at the same time. Since the new delivery company had to make only one early-morning delivery run for both papers, obvious economies were instantly possible. A heavy cost-drain operation turned into a highly profitable business. It was a win for Pacific Press, a win for a new trucking concern, but a definite loss for highly paid unionized drivers.

For years, Americans have eschewed government-run businesses. Not so in Canada. The city of Calgary, however, is considering the American approach. City politicians are asking, "Why is the municipal government trying to manage businesses? Governments on all levels are poor at running businesses."

Calgary politicians are also questioning, "Why don't we privatize our utilities?" Calgary owns three utilities: the municipal electrical service, waterworks, and sewer services. They estimate that their utilities would sell for more than $800 million. This windfall would erase from the account books the city's long-standing, $500 million debt and, at the same time, produce $511 million to spend in capital improvements. Have the lights gone on again all over Calgary?

The timing is right, according to RBC Dominion Securities, the company that broached the idea to Calgary City Council. RBC completed a large $851 million privatization of Nova Scotia Power Inc. in 1992, and now senses that "the convergence of investor appetite, fiscal constraints, and attractive assets make this an opportune time to explore this initiative." Smart move by RBC. Calgary City Council has to agree to pay RBC $200,000 for a feasibility study of the privatization prospect. Yet, as RBC's initial report noted, the elimination of tax-supported debt would exceed the loss of revenue from the utilities.

Watch the spread of outsourcing and privatization. You've only seen the start of how these trends will change our futures.

Everyone is an Inventor

After giving so many lectures about the necessity of changing for future survival, I figured it was time to come up with a totally new product. By good fortune and a smart idea, I met the challenge in three days. In the past it would have taken months to create a new product, but on the cusp of an electronic age this is no longer the case.

Here's the story of my latest invention. For the last decade, I have been writing a column called "Dr. Tomorrow," which is syndicated in 40 publications. Every few years, I organize my columns into collections that I call "books." My books are really texts on computer disks. Each disk holds the contents of an entire manuscript. The only thing that's missing is paper and binding.

Until now, my books have been available in two formats only: on computer disks and on CD-ROM disks. Initially, I supplied them on 5.25-inch disks and then on 3.5-inch computer disks in either Macintosh or IBM/clone formats. The CD-ROM format came a bit later. Over time, my columns filled a ten-volume computer-disk set.

My goal in inventing a new product was to use an old item — hundreds of my columns on ten computer disks — to produce a new one. As I was developing my idea, a new issue of *MacWorld*, a leading computer magazine, arrived on my desk. There was an advertisement in the magazine for new "floptical" disk drives. These new computer drives, which store, copy, and retrieve data were advertised at a price only slightly more costly than the best traditional standard drives. The new drive had the capability of processing both the traditional-format disks and the new 21-megabyte disk format. The new disks could hold more than 20 times the capacity of previous disks.

A possibility was emerging.

Using the toll-free American 800 telephone number, I got confirmation of the current price and ordered the disk drive, which arrived from California within 48 hours. I immediately installed it.

Within 24 hours, I had all ten of my previous volumes copied on a single floptical disk in both English and Spanish. With the 20 volumes in two languages on a single disk, fresh opportunities emerged. The disk was now an educational tool because the text could be split-screened and made to appear in two languages, an innovative, simple way to study another tongue. It took two more hours to have the new product reproduced on the very computer which I had used to write my columns. The price of the new disks, initially $36 each, dropped to $21 within two months as sales of the new product mounted. Soon, other advantages of the disk became apparent. My regular ten-volume set of computer disks weighs over 500 grams and costs up to $9 to mail across the country; my new, single, super-high 21-megabyte density disk, with the same dimensions as earlier disks, weighs but 63 grams and costs only 86 cents to mail, a saving of 90 percent over previous postage costs.

The advantages of technology are endless. Once a person jumps aboard the bulldozer of change, he or she gets used to thinking differently. My books are currently being translated into *kanji*, the Chinese characters readable by people who speak either Cantonese or Mandarin. This gives me entrée to the immense market of China. Because of the quantity of data the new disks can hold, all ten volumes will fit on the same disk in the new Chinese format. Now the disk is a multiple-language learning tool! Furthermore, using an almost-free, public-domain software program like Smooth Talker, or even the reasonably priced Mac Talker ($39), my books can now read themselves aloud in a male, female, or robotic voice in English, Spanish, or Chinese.

At no time in the past could a product be developed so fast. This example shows why it's important to move into the crystal lane which has replaced the old fast-lane. Those unwilling to capitalize on the latest developments face slipping into the land of the technopeasant as new technologies, products, and services change the way the world moves.

Future Feed

As old institutions and industries change around us, new options and opportunities arise. Are you in the food industry? If so, perhaps one day soon you may become an ostrich farmer. You do not have to be a food scientist or an agricultural economist to see why anyone would want to raise cattle when he or she could raise ostriches. During the last ten years, 3,000 ostrich ranches have sprung up in the United States, and since 1987 more Canadians than ever have been moving into this lucrative field. In Alberta alone, there are now more than 200 ostrich ranches.

Check out the facts for yourself. The following tables illustrate the advantages of raising ostriches.

Table 1: The Ostrich Compared to the Cow

	Ostrich	*Cow*
Gestation/incubation period	42 days	9 months
Number of offspring	25 chicks	1 calf
Sale as Breed Stock at 3 months	$2,500 x 25 chicks @ 120 lb each = $62,500	500 lb @ $1 per lb = $500
Price of Dressed Meat	3,000 lb x $5.00 per lb = $15,000	500 lb x $1.40 per lb = $700

Table 2: The Advantage of Ostrich Meat*

Type	Cholesterol	Calories	Fat	Protein
Ostrich	54.1	82.5	.85	18.6
Chicken (thigh)	70.6	96.6	3.30	16.7
Chicken (breast)	54.4	93.5	1.02	19.6
Turkey	62.1	88.4	1.36	18.9
Beef (bottom Round)	55.3	191.3	13.30	16.9

*Sampled weight 85 grams raw meat.

An ostrich chick usually grows one foot each month for nine months. It may live 81 years, although at that age its running speed of 45 miles an hour does slow down. Ostriches are vegetarians and eat seven pounds of food a day. They have the largest eyes of any land animal and are the only bird with just two toes. Ostriches produce 1.5 pounds of feathers each season and an ostrich egg is the largest-size egg, though it is the smallest in relation to the bird's size.

The "backward" rancher in South Africa has been in the ostrich business since 1857. When one, three- to four-pound ostrich egg can feed as many people as 25 chicken eggs can, and an ostrich hen can lay more than 100 eggs annually for 40 years, you get the yolk—even though it does take 45 minutes to hard-boil an ostrich egg. Gourmet meat, fine-quality leather, and lovely feathers worth almost three times their weight in gold (up to $1,000 a pound) makes raising ostriches a business that sparkles.

Magic Renewal

To see the future, we sometimes have to look into the past. Well before the Stone Age, magic ran the world. Magical acts calmed people's fear of their jungle-dark, technologically starved planet. With a bit of magic, people could deal with a static but unknown environment. Those people who could work, control, or create magic were important in prehistoric times. Perhaps if we accept that there is a logical, coherent belief system behind magic, we might relieve some of today's urban stresses.

Before the advent of logic, fire, the wheel, and language, people developed rituals, a dance to the rain gods, for example. They also tried to locate something in the jungle that could transport them into another world so that they might personally meet the gods. That "something" could have been yage, the South American vine; hemp, the hallucinogen of India; the mushrooms of the Aztecs; the yam of Papua New Guinea; the fishing magic of the Trobriand islanders; or the peyote cactus buttons of the American Indians. They all served a purpose. Some anthropologists and pharmacologists believe these substances helped people cope with the world better than what we rely on today—alcohol, caffeine, nicotine, and cocaine, and soap operas.

I lived with the voodooists in Haiti for two years, and learned their patterns of nonverbal communication. I now see things in our supposedly civilized society that aren't much different from life in a jungle. From a tropical mamba, I received more effective medical treatment than from a scientifically trained Western doctor. After all, medical estimates say that at least 25 percent of modern medicines are derived from jungle sources.

In the late-nineteenth and early-twentieth centuries, Sir Edward Tylor and Sir James Frazer championed the anthropological theory that magic can be regarded as instances of early or pseudoscientific research. Magic sees a connection between cause and effect. Frazer observed that the principle is "like producing like." In other words, an effect resembles its cause, and things that were once in contact continue to be in contact even after physical contact has ended. I could list a hundred things that work that way today—the stock market, for example.

In most parts of the world, magic has been succeeded by religion. But the winds of change, particularly in some parts of Western society, are blowing new modes of thinking into the minds of many. There is much for us to learn from people who have yet to reach our level of culture and from those who in many ways have bypassed it.

A Trip Through Technology

Before looking at products of tomorrow, read through the following list of inventions which have allowed us to travel through history, from the agricultural age to the end of the industrial age. The river of change continues to accelerate relentlessly and now the early waves of the communications age are lapping at the old crumbling sand castles of recent decades. Soon our culture will be unrecognizable. Time has a habit of changing things beyond the familiar.

For many, an impetus to invent came from Johannes Gutenberg, who created the printing press. His invention inspired others to explore new terrain and to pass on their knowledge. During the industrial age, inventors provided life-improving developments. Since the seventeenth century there's been such a torrent of inventions that we have taken most of them for granted. Take a look at the list of technological items, all of which have altered our lives irrevocably:

• **Telescope:** Created by Dutchman Johann Lippershey in 1608.

• **Submarine:** Dutchman Cornelius Drebbel successfully navigated a submerged boat with 12 rowers on board in England's Thames River in the seventeenth century.

• **Automobile:** Nicholas-Joseph Cugnot of France

built the first automobile in 1770.

• **False Teeth:** The first set of porcelain dentures was made by Alexis Dachateau near Paris in 1770, but a set of false teeth, retrieved from a field in Switzerland, is believed to date from the fifteenth century.

• **Spring Sail:** Designed by Andrew Meikle in 1772, the Spring Sail was the most powerful type of windmill to appear in England since its invention in the twelfth century.

• **Patent Sail:** Another windmill design by Sir William Cubilt of Norfolk, England, followed in 1807.

• **Steam Engine:** The first working steam engine was invented by Thomas Newcomen in Staffordshire, England, in 1712. Scotsman James Watt built the first steam engine with a separate condenser in 1765. He also built the first double-acting engine in 1782.

• **Steamboat:** The Marquis Claude François Dorothée de Jouffroy d'Abbans conducted the first trial run on the Saône River from Lyon to the Isle Barbe on July 15, 1783.

• **Balloon:** The hot air balloon was invented by Joseph and Etienne Montgolfier on June 5, 1783. Its first ascension took place near Lyon, France.

• **Telegraph:** Claude Chappe of France developed the first serviceable device, in the form of a semaphore, in 1792.

• **Pith-Ball Telegraph:** A form of the acoustic telegraph was invented by Karl Steinheil in 1836.

• **Original Computer:** An analytical engine, designed and built by Charles Babbage at Cambridge University in 1812, was the forerunner of the modern computer.

- **Photograph:** We owe this one to French amateur scientist Joseph Nicephore of Nice in the spring of 1816.

- **Transoceanic Steamship:** The first steamship to cross the Atlantic was the *Savannah*, departing from New York for Ireland in 1818.

- **Electric Telegraph System:** The first practical electrical system was produced in England by Sir William Fothergill Cooke and Sir Charles Wheatstone in 1837.

- **Electric Telegraph:** American Samuel Morse is credited with inventing this in 1832; he gave a private demonstration of its capability in 1837.

- **Production Assembly Line:** Developed by Elisha King Root and Samuel Colt of Hartford, Connecticut, in 1848.

- **Dirigible:** Credited to Frenchman Henri Giffard in 1852.

- **Rotary Power Printing:** A steam-operated mechanical printing press by Friedrich Koenig of Germany was demonstrated in London in 1811. The first rotary press built by an American, William Bullock, appeared in 1863.

- **Telephone:** The first person to demonstrate rudimentary transmission in Germany in 1863 was Philipp Reis. Alexander Graham Bell undertook his more successful operation in 1876.

- **Typewriter:** Christopher Scholes, Carlos Glidden, and Latham Soule developed the modern commercial form of the typewriter in Milwaukee in 1868.

- **Trans-Atlantic Cable:** Professor William Thompson,

working for American Cyrus W. Field, who formed the Atlantic Telegraph Company, is credited with this early development in 1866.

- **Lightbulb:** Thomas Alva Edison brought light to the world in 1879 at Menlo Park, East Orange, New Jersey.

- **Motion Pictures:** Cinematography, the principle on which motion pictures are based, was first demonstrated in England by Dr. Peter Mark Roget in 1824. A Belgian, J.A. Plateau, with his Phenakistiscope, provided a moving image in 1833. In Paris, Auguste and Louis Lumière perfected the idea, and it was shown publicly on December 28, 1895.

- **Wireless Telegraph:** Guglielmo Marchese Marconi made contact between France and England in 1899, and his world-renowned transmission between Cornwall, England, and St. John's, Newfoundland, occurred in 1901.

- **Airplane:** Bicycle mechanics Orville and Wilbur Wright first flew their machine on December 17, 1903, at Kitty Hawk, South Carolina.

- **Parachute:** The first human to drop from a balloon was Frenchman A.J. Garnerin over Paris in 1797. First to drop from an airplane was American Albert Barry over St. Louis, Missouri, March 1, 1912.

- **Artificial Kidney:** Americans John J. Able, L.G. Rowntree, and B.B. Turner developed this invention in 1913. The first person to test the artificial kidney on humans was Dutchman Willem Kolff in 1945.

- **Scuba Gear:** This device for diving was patented by William James on May 31, 1925.

- **Snowmobile:** The first small motorized ski-sled was built by Wisconsin storekeeper Carl Eliason in 1927.
- **Satellite Orbit:** First conceived by science-fiction author Arthur C. Clarke and presented in the 1945 article "Extra Terrestrial Relays" published in *Wireless World.*
- **Magnetic Resonance Image Scanner:** Principle of electron spin resonance (ESR) by Zavoiski in 1945. Discovery of nuclear magnetic resonance (NMR) by Purcell, Pound, and Torrey of Harvard University, and by Block, Hansen, and Packard of Stanford University in 1946.
- **Electronic Computer:** The ENIAC computer designed by J. Presper Eckert and Jon W. Mauchy of the University of Pennsylvania was completed in 1945. The first commercially available computer was the UNIVAC built by Eckert for Mauchy Computer Company founded in 1946. The EDVAC computer was completed in 1952. The completion of the ISA computer was a joint venture between Princeton's Institute of Advanced Studies and the Moore School in 1952.
- **Hovercraft:** Invented by English engineer Christopher Cockerell in 1950.
- **Computer Hard Drive:** Reynold Johnston of IBM England developed the spinning disk and hard disk in 1955.
- **Heart-Lung Machine:** First successful application was made by John H. Gibbon in the United States on May 6, 1953.
- **Space Shuttle:** *Sputnik*, No. 1, was launched

October 4, 1957, by the USSR. First man in orbit was Soviet cosmonaut Yuri Gagarin, April 12, 1961.

- **Satellite Dish:** On September 14, 1976, Taylor Howard of Stanford University invented the first satellite dish built for personal use.
- **Computer Disk:** Alan Shugart developed the eight-inch plastic disk in the late 1960s.
- **CAT-Scanner:** Developed by Alan Cormick and Godfrey Honsfield in 1962.
- **Gene-Splicing:** A preliminary work on the topic was published by Mike Smith, University of British Columbia, in 1978; a definitive paper on the subject was produced in 1982.
- **Artificial Heart/Mechanical Heart:** Invented by Robert K. Jarvik at the University of Utah. The first artificial heart implant, the Jarvik 7, occurred on December 2, 1982.
- **High-Speed Ferry:** *Supercat* was the first such ferry to be launched by the British Hoverspeed Company in 1990.

What will be the next invention that will alter our lives? Technology will tell. We won't have to wait long for tomorrow's discoveries as the rate of change is ever accelerating. Today's digirati are in the constant process of revolutionizing life as we know it.

Metal Matters

In the Witwatersrand area of the Transvaal in South Africa, unmined reserves of gold, estimated to be 500 million troy ounces (about 15 billion grams), still await the miner's claw. This accounts for about half the earth's unmined reserves of gold. Since the beginning of this century, South Africa has prospered because of gold and its sister substance, platinum. Today, political instability in South Africa threatens the previously guaranteed source of 50 percent of the world's production of gold.

In human travel along the river of time, gold has been wealth. Aside from some rare artifacts carved from the metal, jewelry, and gold leaf, it has been used almost exclusively as a currency or a currency reserve. But as the main source of the metal appears endangered, new uses for gold have materialized.

Gold is in demand in the exploding computer industry for microelectrical circuits, and as a heat shield to prevent the transfer of infrared radiation. It is used in modern manufacturing to cover bearings in corrosive atmospheres, or as a plating on equipment subject to corrosive fluids or vapors. Such uses seem a solid trend, at least in the immediate future. Because of its lack of toxicity and general compatibility with human biology, gold has become almost indispensable in dentistry and medicine, although in these areas modern plastics and ceramics threaten continuing consumption of the metal.

There are sound economic reasons to explain why gold could once again become the first choice for all investors. There are many ways to store and control gold: in the gold certificates of banks, in the gold shares of major gold-mining companies, and in ornate jewelry. Many people in India have no bank accounts, safe-deposit boxes, or the security protection of personal vaults. Walk along any Indian street and you will see women who wear traditionally safe portable banks around their necks, wrists, ankles, and fingers in the form of bracelets, bangles, rings, and so on.

Though gold is increasing in value, even greater potential lies in the price of platinum. In 1920, platinum was about eight times more than gold; today it is running only 5 percent above the price of gold. In the near future, an upward price move is indicated. One of the reasons for this is that not much platinum is left in the earth. The same is true of other members of the platinum family: ruthenium, rhodium, palladium, osmium, iridium. (Platinum is the most common of these rare elements, found in about one-millionth of 1 percent of the earth's crust.) South Africa provides about 80 percent of the world supply of platinum. The milling and reduction process of platinum is much more complicated and lengthy than it is for gold. Few people are aware of the platinum potential because the metal is not as well-known or as long-respected as gold.

Europeans discovered platinum in 1735, but pre-Columbian Indians had used it for centuries. New developments exploit platinum's unusual characteristics. An alloy of 76.7 percent platinum and 23.3 percent cobalt forms an extremely powerful magnet which someday may be in substantial demand for levitational transportation, such as the magnetic levitation trains now running in Germany and Japan. It is already used for the coating of missile cones and jet-engine fuel nozzles. Platinum "dust" makes an almost perfect catalyst applied largely in the petrochemical industry. Platinum testing continues for potential use in fuel cells and with antipollution devices for automobiles. The metal is employed in such sophisticated scientific searches as shadow casting, a process associated with electron-tunneling microscopes. Various new applications for this unusual metal keep appearing, especially in the newer, more sophisticated fields of high technology.

Given the choice between backing gold or platinum, my bet is on the platinum potential.

No-Stick Paint

Japanese innovators keep coming up with thousands of new developments. In the early 1990s, the Sony Corporation alone produced and marketed more than 1,800 new products.

One of the latest products from Japan is a new repellent that is almost 50 percent more effective in resisting water than similar products.

Here's how the repellent was invented. During the winters of 1992 and 1993, Japan's Nippon Telephone & Telegraph (NTT) was experiencing trouble with above-ground phone lines, because of snow sticking to wireless relay station antennae in the Hida Mountains. In order to solve their problem, NTT rapidly developed a new paint. Snow could not stick to any surfaces covered in the material. It became apparent that this new coating represented a breakthrough in the field of repellents. Today, the repellent's applications are diverse; it can be used on telecommunications devices like antennae, transportation devices like ships' hulls, mountain-chair and cable-car lifts, funicular railway lines, road and railway tunnels, all permanent outdoor structures, even inflatable stadiums. On ships at anchor, the material could retard the growth of barnacle colonies and other crustaceans. The repellent could also be used on a variety of vehicles, sports equipment, home hardware, and other situations where corrosion resistance is essential. When applied to roofs with a slant of at least 45 degrees, the repellent prevents snow from accumulating. Could Canada ever use it!

Conventional water-repellent materials have, NTT says, a water-contact angle of roughly 100 degrees. Their material exceeds 145 degrees, as a result of remarkably weak interaction between the coating surface and water.

The uniform coating of fine fluorine-compound particles combines with the low surface-free energy of the medium coating surface. Put simply, water rolls off anything painted with the NTT material.

Last winter, NTT's water-repellent paint was applied to wireless antennae. Results confirmed expectations. The coating resisted snow to a significant degree. Further testing, evaluation, and possible expansions are continuing—to achieve stability, durability, and abrasion resistance to match commercial needs. Further development and marketing will be handled through Advance Technology Corporation and Advanced Film Technology Inc., both NTT subsidiaries.

NTT is currently comparing the long-term effects of ultraviolet sun rays, which accelerate deterioration, with the effects of normal sunlight. Already the company has evidence that the new repellent can be maintained for at least 20 years in direct exposure to outdoor sunlight.

The super water-repellent is not harmful to humans. "It neither enters nor accumulates in the human body, unlike organic mercury. It does not harm the ozone layer, nor is it known to cause any other environmental problems as it uses a fluorine compound rather than a volatile substance such as Freon," says an NTT spokesperson. Fine particles that disperse light gives the product a naturally white color. It can be mixed with pigment or paint and it has no odor.

Before splitting into several companies, NTT was twice the size of General Motors, IBM, AT&T, and a dozen other large companies combined. NTT divided so that each of its segments could continue to grow. Unquestionably, we'll be hearing more about NTT companies in the future.

Eternally Yours

When I autograph one of my books these days, I am secure in the knowledge that, long after I am gone, my signature can always be proven to be authentic. No counterfeiter can duplicate it. No forger can withstand an investigation of his or her handiwork. What provides this confidence that no one in the past could ever enjoy? DNA Art Guard!

Every time I sign my name with my special pen and innovative ink, my signature is sacrosanct. Why? The ink contains my own personal genetic code, my own DNA. No one else's can match it.

Everyone on the planet, except for identical twins, has his or her own DNA, the only identification element known to forensic science that is impossible to duplicate without the original formula. It is about the only thing that can provide *positive* personal identification. Think of how the sale of forged paintings could have been avoided had every masterpiece been positively identified as authentic.

DNA Art Guard was introduced and used for the first time on a literary work in Toronto in March 1995. I was selected by Art Guard to introduce the invention to the senior corporate executives who attended the Padulo Institute for Tomorrow's "Survival Course for the 21st Century CEO." Naturally, the new pen and ink was a hit. Executives instantly saw the advantages of having some definitive way to ensure, for all time, that every check, contract, or other important document signed in any country of the world could be proven to bear the signature of the signee. In the future, all my print books, computer disks, and CD-ROMs will carry my DNA-coded signature.

The anticounterfeiting system was created and developed by DNA Art Guard Inc. of Los Angeles. The system includes a scanner and detectors that can provide immediate verification of authenticity. Using state-of-the-art DNA and biological markers in combination with unique illumination, the system provides an immediate and irrefutable verification of authenticity. Bonded with rare chemical materials, this biochemical combination lends itself to visual or electronic detection. The atomically biased biochemistry reacts to excitation by a single wavelength of energy emitted by an Art Guard energy source that is similar to x-ray detection. The resultant "flashback" can be observed visually or detected invisibly. The biochemistry has its own emission spectra, frequency, and intensity. This chemical "fingerprint" is generally acknowledged by courts worldwide as verified evidence of source. Art Guard holds international rights to imprint DNA (and all other biological markers), by covert yet detectable means, as identification.

As the leading method to prevent forgeries with fine art, DNA Art Guard will become *de rigueur*. Art galleries lacking such a system to authenticate art will find their insurance rates increasing and client confidence eroding, as knowledge of the system becomes widespread.

What's next? Expect DNA phone cards, patented pharmaceutical, stocks, bonds, passports, holograms, auto parts, luggage, jewelry, computer software, sports equipment, and more—all Art Guarded!

Bodycam

Imagine having a "bodycam," a pocket-size television camera with a separate transmitter (incorporating an audio subcarrier) combined with a wearable power source. It would be the perfect armament for the arsenal of video vigilantes. Can you imagine what would have happened had Rodney King's cameraman used body-cams? What if the police had used them? Most likely, the Rodney King incident wouldn't have occurred, had the police known that a senior officer was recording the entire chase.

Today, the bodycam—an untethered color television camera that transmits from your pocket—already exists! At one inch thick, it is the smallest and lightest video camera in the world. When I heard about it, I liked the idea so much I bought one sight unseen.

The new camera is the latest from Supercircuits of Austin, Texas, the manufacturers of the PC-4 Supermini four-ounce color video camera and the PC-3 1.32-ounce microscopic version. Not only is the PC-4 small (3 1/8-inch wide x 3 7/8-inch high x 1-inch deep), it has 310 lines of resolution. And it runs on 12 volts, with low power consumption.

Capable of capturing pictures with only two lux (one candle power per lux), it will record an image with almost any amount of light. Wide-angle and other lenses are available. The camera's output is standard NTSC, and it can transmit (9-volt ATV) from any vehicle or model flying machine. The PC-3 model, although much lighter (measuring 1 7/8-inch x 2 7/8-inch x 1-inch), does not yet have the higher resolution or color of the PC-4 version. Both models have a built-in iris for automatic exposure. A transmitter is available at a reasonable extra cost. Like other modern camcorders, both the PC-3 and PC-4 have a pack of extras available for the real aficionados: optional lens, special cases, and so forth.

The bodycam will generate new applications that will astound the marketplace: computer imaging, "toyvision," robotics, and police surveillance. Think of what you can do with this unit the next time you go bungee-jumping, skydiving, driving, rock-climbing, or golfing. Or imagine wearing a "hatcam" to your next party. Coming soon: a video camera inside your body!

Conclusion: Comfort in Chaos

Pay attention to the possibilities that are available when you keep in touch with change. Let me give you a few examples.

The United States military spent billions of dollars developing the Stealth bomber. At first, it worked great. No radar could pick up the aircraft, no matter where it flew. Then one day, two Australians renovated an old war-surplus weather-radar system that was designed to detect vortices, like tornadoes. The Aussies turned the system on its side and altered the machinery so that it would track horizontal tornadoes at high, instead of low, altitudes. They pointed their modified radar system a couple of miles behind a Stealth aircraft. It picked up the bomber's speed, direction, altitude, and changes en route.

In the United States, the military developed the Global Position Indicator (GPI) system. By using this hand-held GPI instrument, a soldier could find a position, which four satellites could verify within seconds. The GPI worked until civilian programmers, smarter than those in the American military, developed more sophisticated algorithms to provide near-military accuracy at a fraction of the cost. The military should have learned that anything they can do, civilians can do better and cheaper.

In the early 1970s, an Oklahoman named Bob Cooper was intrigued by the news that an earthbound satellite dish could pick up signals emanating from communications devices located at an altitude of 22,300 miles over the equator. Lacking the required government authorization and access to the millions of dollars needed to construct such highly technical apparatus, Cooper went to the local grocery store and picked up a couple of dollars' worth of aluminum foil. With his sheets of foil and a rustic, shield-shaped device, he built his home "dish." For pennies he did what governments were doing for millions.

True, the initial picture Cooper picked up wouldn't have won an Oscar for its technological excellence. However, it did work, improvements rapidly followed, and the whole backyard–satellite–dish phenomenon followed. Thousands of men and women found employment in an exciting, grassroots industry that was expanding rapidly. Millions of technologically-minded people worldwide moved, at least intellectually, into the space age and far ahead of experts, acquiring information from traditional sources. Cooper eventually retired in the Caribbean, and turned his battery of dishes into a cable company.

If surplus junk in Australia can allow two outbackers with incentive to accomplish what was only believed possible with a government's expenditure of millions, if not billions, anything is possible. Just remember how quick Cooper was to lead the way with satellite dishes. Thousands of opportunities are out there today for enterprising individuals. If a company, an industry, or an idea has been around for ten years, look elsewhere. Let traditional workers fill mundane, hourly-paid positions. Look for the unknown. That's where the future lies.

There are exceptions to every generalization. I never hesitate to look at old patents, ideas that didn't make it into production over the last hundred years. The world was different in those days. Now, with improved materials and new knowledge, some of those neglected ideas might work. Keep looking.

The most lucrative information mine of tomorrow lies in chaos. Discover the elegant order underlying chaos. Its pattern cannot be taught.

Appendix

Navigating in Cyberspace on CD-ROM

Now that you have read *Navigating in Cyberspace* in its Gutenberg format, be sure to take a look at it on CD-ROM. This brand-new product offers an interactive, electronic presentation of my latest thoughts on the currents of change that are coursing through the world today.

Much more than a book text on screen, this CD-ROM will allow you to enjoy graphics, text, sights, and sounds!

Simply pop the disk into a CD-ROM reader. You will see, hear, and enjoy a wealth of information including my television, audio, and print interviews; the texts of two of my books (*The Last Book You'll Ever Read* and *Navigating in Cyberspace*); clips from my CD-ROM, *Dr. Tomorrow's Cyberspace University*; and highlights of the first "Survival Course for the 21st Century CEO" sponsored by the

Padulo Institute for Tomorrow.

The disk is a hybrid CD-ROM so it can be used on IBM compatible computers and the Apple Macintosh. The text of *Navigating in Cyberspace* is offered in ASCII text format for IBM-compatible computers. You can use any text editor to access these files on your personal computer.

A special stand-alone version of *Navigating* is provided for Macintosh owners in addition to the text files. To use this version of the book you will require a Macintosh with at least four megabytes of available RAM memory and a color monitor. Apple's Quicktime extension is also required if you wish to see the short video clips available on the disk. Once you open up the CD-ROM, see the "read me" file for further instructions.

Frank Ogden

You have **read** his words...now **hear** him speak!

Frank Ogden
Dr. Tomorrow™
is one of the most popular speakers
in the world today.
Frank addresses groups of all sorts.
He delivers keynote addresses...makes speeches...
lectures...leads discussions...hosts executive retreats...
and conducts senior-management and business survival
seminars for the ever-changing world of business.
His presentations are dramatic...and inspiring!
For information about how to book
one of his personal appearances,
contact:

The National Speakers Bureau

In Canada: 1 (800) 661-4110
Elsewhere: 1 (604) 224-2384
Fax: 1 (604) 224-8906
E-mail: speakers@nsb.com

The page design of *Navigating in Cyberspace* was designed by Peter Enneson and James Ireland using Quark Express software. The body text is set in Adobe Garamond, a revival of Claude Garamond's mid 16th-century type designs. Adobe Garamond was drawn by Robert Simlach and issued as a postscript font by Adobe Inc. in 1989. Chapter headings, secondary headings, running heads and folios were set in the Emigré typeface Modula, created by Zuzana Licko in 1986.